A FIRST STAMP ALBUM
FOR BEGINNERS

D1314208

ROBERT OBOJSKI

Revised and Enlarged by the
Staff of Dover Publications

Dover Publications, Inc.
Mineola, New York

Bibliographical Note

A First Stamp Album for Beginners published in 2004, is a revised edition of
the work first published by Dover Publications, Inc., in 1984.

International Standard Book Number
ISBN-13: 978-0-486-44113-9
ISBN-10: 0-486-44113-X

Manufactured in the United States by Courier Corporation
44113X03
www.doverpublications.com

Introduction

Welcome to the exciting hobby of stamp collecting! You are now part of a large group of people from all over the world who share a lively interest in the beauty and history of postage stamps. The fact that stamp collecting has long been the most popular hobby in the world, with over 16 million enthusiasts in the United States alone, is a good indication of how much fascination and appeal these colorful little pieces of gummed paper exert. Another is the fact that many collectors are adults who became interested in the hobby when they were children and have found it a stimulating and fun activity throughout their lives. The more they learn about the world of postage stamps, the more enjoyment they get from each new addition to their collection. Each new stamp from a faraway place brings to the collector some of the excitement and adventure of foreign travel, and a curiosity to learn more about that country—where is it, how large is it, how old is it, how many people live there, what languages do its citizens speak, what is life there like, and so forth. No doubt you will quickly fall under the spell of postage stamps yourself, and become a *philatelist*, a fancier word for stamp collector.

The History of Stamp Collecting in a Nutshell

The hobby of stamp collecting began soon after the first adhesive (gummed-back) postage stamp was issued by Great Britain in 1840, over 160 years ago. Because it cost only one penny and showed a profile portrait of the then twenty-one-year-old Queen Victoria on a black

Figure 1. The first true postage stamp ever issued—the famous Penny Black, which dates from 1840.

background, this now very famous stamp is known as the Penny Black. It's so old, and therefore rare and expensive, you're not very likely to come across one soon, but be on the lookout anyway. Many fabulously rare stamps have been found by amateur collectors purely by chance. In some ways stamp collecting is a little like playing detective!

After Great Britain issued the Penny Black, other countries quickly realized that issuing stamps was a very good way to pay for the costs of running a public postal system. Up until that time, letter delivery systems were mostly in private hands and very expensive—way beyond the means of the average citizen. There was also a good deal of confusion and not a little dishonesty in the earlier systems; sometimes the person sending a letter prepaid the delivery charges, and sometimes letters were sent "collect," meaning that the person receiving it was expected to pay for its delivery. Unfortunately, many clever people quickly learned how to cheat the system; they would put their message in a simple code on the envelope itself, as part of the address, and then send it collect. The person receiving it would glance at the envelope, quickly decipher the code—thereby receiving the message— and then refuse to accept the letter or pay the expensive delivery charges! Cheap postage did away with these abuses of the system and led to fast, efficient mail-delivery systems all over the world.

An indication of the postage stamp's success is that 30 years after the Penny Black was issued a total of over 7,000 different stamps were being issued by many countries. The number of different stamps being issued doubled by the year 1914, and nowadays well over 15,000 different stamps are issued each year by every government in the world. It has been estimated that altogether more than 400,000 different adhesive postal stamps have been issued to date!

With such a vast number of stamps in existence, it is impossible for any one collector to have a complete collection, containing a specimen of every stamp ever issued. Nevertheless some serious philatelists have tried for completeness and have spent enormous fortunes in their search for rare items to fill the empty spaces in their bulging albums. But most collectors eventually find it more interesting to begin to specialize in one or two kinds or varieties of stamps, thereby making it at least within the realm of possibility to form a complete collection. Some concentrate on stamps from a single country; others collect only stamps with pictures of birds on them, or flowers, or famous women, or renowned scientists, or airplanes, or boats. The list of possible topical specialties is endless.

Others decide to limit their collection to stamps of unusual shapes, say diamond or triangular, while others focus on stamps with printing errors (upside down pictures, for instance) or airmail stamps. A particularly interesting special type is the commemorative, a stamp issued to honor a person or to mark the anniversary of an important event.

Another form of specialization would be to limit one's collection to *mint* stamps, stamps that have never seen postal duty and thus have not been cancelled. Cancellation is the process of imprinting black lines over stamps when a letter is processed at the post office, in order to prevent their being used over again. In the early years of stamp production the cancellation process was not perfect, and it was possible for people to "clean" stamps and reuse them over and over, thereby causing great financial problems for the postal systems.

Where to Begin

The stamp album you now have is ideal for beginning collectors. It pictures over 1,100 quite easy-to-find stamps from almost 200 different countries. When you find a stamp that looks like one shown, place it right over the illustration. Double-check, though, to make sure the stamp is an *exact* match to the picture – for instance, that the *denomination* (amount of money the stamp sold for in the post office when it was first issued) is the same. The only differences between the stamps you find and those pictured should be (1) that the actual stamps are printed in colors whereas all the pictures in this album are in black and white, and (2) that the actual stamps are also slightly larger (about 10 per cent) than the pictured ones.

Within the space devoted to the 195 countries (technically called *issuing authorities*) there are also many blank boxes where you can put stamps from that nation which are not pictured. Altogether there are spaces for more than 2,350 stamps in the main part of the album (pages 1–65) and room for 200 more in the extra blank

pages at the end that you can use for whatever purpose you decide is appropriate. Perhaps you'll want to use these pages to begin a specialized collection of your own.

If you are careful to put your stamps in the album in just the way we describe below, you'll be able to remove them easily any time you want and perhaps eventually put them in a larger album picturing every stamp ever issued in the whole world! You'll have to save about $50, though, in order to buy such a complete album.

How to Obtain Stamps Cheaply

One of the nicest things about stamp collecting is that it need not be an expensive hobby. In fact you can get a lot of interesting stamps absolutely free! Just let your relatives, friends and neighbors know that you are starting a collection and you'll find that they will be glad to give you all the stamps they receive on their mail. Even if you get only three or four people to help you, you'll quickly gather a large number of stamps.

Another source of free stamps is other stamp collectors. All collectors accumulate duplicates, extra copies of stamps. After examining all the copies he has of a particular stamp and saving the cleanest and freshest-looking one for his own collection, every collector is eager to trade the others for stamps he does not yet own. Perhaps there is a stamp collecting club at your school; if so, join it and have fun learning about stamps and their history and meet people who will be interested in swapping stamps with you.

Packages of stamps can be purchased at dime stores, department stores and hobby shops. You can get quite a large number of stamps for a dollar or less, but generally the more stamps you get for your money, the lower the quality will be. In other words, the "bargain" packages with lots of stamps in them will tend to have rather worn, very common stamps, and lots of duplicates. Other, slightly more expensive, packages, or packages selling for the same price but containing fewer stamps, will have better quality stamps and fewer duplicates.

Using This Album

In order to use this album, you have to understand how it is organized. Actually it's set up much like almost every other stamp album, even the most complete ones. The countries or issuing authorities are arranged alphabetically according to their names in the English language, except that the United States comes first, followed by the United Nations, and countries that were once territories, colonies or possessions of England, Holland, France or other countries are generally located following the "mother country."

You'll notice that the countries in this album are numbered 1 (United States) through 195 (Yemen Arab Republic). These little numbers that appear just above and to the left of each country's name will be very useful to you; they'll make it possible for you to quickly locate exactly where to place any stamp you may come across!

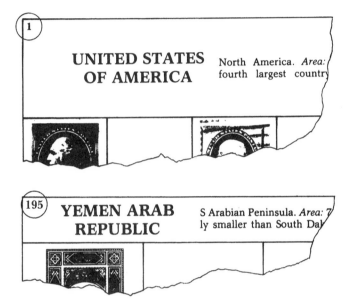

Figure 2. The numbers circled in this illustration are the ones referred to in the Stamp Identifier Table.

We'll give two examples to show how easy it is to decide the right place to put almost any stamp you find, even very "mysterious" ones. Let's suppose you have obtained the two stamps pictured below. The first thing to do is study each one carefully to try to discover what the most prominent word or words on it are. The largest word on the stamp on the left is certainly "Österreich." Turn to the alphabetically arranged Stamp Iden-

Figure 3. Two stamps you can easily identify using the Stamp Identifier Table.

tifier Table (pages viii–x) and look in the O's for Österreich. You'll quickly find it, followed by the number 10. Thumb through the album keeping your eyes on the little numbers above and to the left of the names of the countries until you come to number 10 on page 14. You'll find that the German-speaking country that calls itself Österreich is known in English as Austria!

Now let's look at the stamp on the right. The most prominent words are "Magyar Posta." You'll probably guess that "Posta" means postage, so let's forget it and look up "Magyar" in the Stamp Identifier Table. You'll find that it's number 132, and when you locate that number in the album (page 48), you see it refers to the country known in English as Hungary. This special system of numbers and the Stamp Identifier Table let you identify stamps from all over the world, even stamps issued by countries whose names have changed over the years, without having to know German, Hungarian or any other foreign language.

This is a good time to mention that the only country in the world that doesn't put its name on all its postage is Great Britain. Perhaps this has something to do with the fact that that was the first country to issue postage stamps. But stamps from Great Britain are not hard to identify; indeed, the mere absence of a country's name is your first and best clue to the stamp's being British. Other clues are that British stamps *almost always* (1) include the world words "postage" and "revenue" on them; (2) show a portrait of the king or queen reigning at the time the stamp was issued; and (3) indicate the number of pence the stamp cost by means of the abbreviation "d" (up until the year 1969) or "p." Therefore, if you find a stamp that doesn't seem to have a country's name on it but does carry the words "2d" (twopence) or "4p" (four pence), for example, you can be pretty sure it's from Great Britain.

You'll notice that next to each country's name we've given you some facts about the size of that nation, usually compared to that of one or more of our States; the number of people living there; the language spoken there; the political status (republic, colony, dependency, etc.); the name of the capital city; and the name of the units of currency. This information is given just to whet your appetite; you'll want to learn more about each country whose stamps you encounter, and easy ways of getting additional information are discussed at the end of this introduction.

Another very special feature of this album is that it includes dates of issue for all stamps pictured. Where you see a single year under a picture, it means that that stamp was only issued during that one year. An entry like 1925–1928, on the other hand, means that that stamp was issued over a four-year period. Generally speaking, the longer the period of issue, the more stamps were produced and the less likely they are to be rare. As in most stamp albums, each country's oldest regular issue stamps are shown first and the most recent ones last. Airmail, Special Delivery and other special issues are placed after the regular issues.

The Right Way to Handle and Mount Stamps

Now that you know how this album is arranged and how to identify any stamps that you may find, you're ready to learn the proper way to handle stamps and the correct way to mount them in the album.

Of course, stamp collecting is primarily a hobby that one does for the sheer fun and excitement of it, but there is a monetary or financial aspect to it as well because some stamps are valuable and many are worth at least a few dollars. Any stamp's value is determined partly on the basis of its rarity and partly by its physical condition, so stamp collectors are careful not to damage stamps while handling them. Unfortunately, there have been many cases in which priceless stamps have been rendered worthless by mishandling.

Here are a few important "DO NOTS" to keep firmly in mind:

1. Never cut into a stamp or trim off any part of its perforated edges.

2. Don't separate stamps that are joined together by their original perforations. A block of four stamps, for instance, is often worth more than the same four stamps would be individually.

3. Don't handle stamps any more than you have to. Natural skin oils from your fingers can stain stamps permanently. Most stamp collectors use stamp tongs to handle their stamps. These tongs are very inexpensive and can be purchased in hobby shops and department stores. Never use tweezers; these have sharp points on the ends which will puncture the stamps.

4. Don't leave stamps in direct sunlight for long periods of time. The colors will fade.

Now, here are a few important "DO'S" to remember:

1. There's only one correct way to remove a used postage stamp from an envelope. All other ways will result in damaged stamps.

First, cut off all the envelope except for about a half-inch all around the stamps. Next, soak this piece of envelope with the stamps on it in a clean dish of warm (not hot) water for 15 or 20 minutes, until the glue dissolves and the stamps float off the paper backing. Finally, put the stamps on a piece of blotting paper to

prevent them from curling up. Don't touch them again until they are completely dry.

2. Stamp collectors never use paste or tape to mount their stamps because over a period of time these adhesives will seep through the paper and stain the face of the stamps. They also make it impossible to remove stamps from albums without damaging them. You will want to be able to remove stamps easily because you'll constantly be upgrading your collection, removing some specimens and replacing them with ones of better quality.

Always use special transparent stamp hinges to mount stamps in albums. They are very inexpensive, and you can buy packages of them in any dime store, stationery store or hobby shop. When you are ready to mount a stamp, hold one of the hinges with the adhesive side up, fold it back a little ways as shown in the figure, and then lightly moisten the folded-back part.

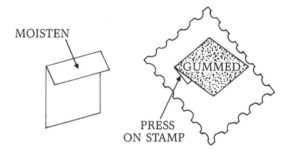

Figure 4. How to mount stamps in an album by means of transparent stamp hinges with gummed backs.

Attach that part of the hinge to the back of the stamp, in the center just below the top perforation. Next lightly moisten the rest of the hinge and affix that part to the album page.

Once the hinge has dried completely you'll be able to detach it from the album and from the stamp easily, without damaging either of them.

Hints on Developing Your New Hobby

Always keep your loose stamps and your stamp album clean and neat. Remember that stamp collecting may turn into a lifelong hobby, lasting years and years. These little pieces of paper we call stamps are fragile and must be treated with care.

The more you learn about stamps and their history, the more enjoyment you will get out of your hobby. When you are working with your stamp collection try to have an atlas, an almanac and perhaps even an encyclopedia nearby, and take the time to find out more about the interesting countries, people, flowers, animals, mountains and other things that stamps will introduce you to. Go to the library and get and read some books on the fascinating hobby of stamp collecting.

You'll also enjoy your hobby much more if you get to know other people who share an interest in stamps. Introduce yourself to the people who run your local hobby shop or stamp-collecting store; they'll be glad to help you and put you in touch with other collectors and perhaps even groups of collectors who meet regularly to talk about the world of postage stamps.

Glossary

We'll close with a short alphabetical list of some special terms stamp collectors use. You'll find that soon you'll be using them too!

Block. An unsevered group of stamps, at least two stamps wide and two stamps high.

Commemorative. A special stamp issued to honor a person or to celebrate an historical event. Commemoratives are usually issued only for short periods of time.

Definitive. A *regular* issue as opposed to a commemorative.

Face value. The original set value of the stamp, its original value for postal purposes.

Gum. The adhesive applied to backs of postage stamps.

Imperforate. A stamp which has no perforations. Most early stamps were imperforate.

Mint stamp. An unused stamp in perfect condition, looking as though it were just purchased at the post office with fresh color, full gum adhesive on the back and all perforations intact.

Pair. Two unsevered stamps.

Pane. An intact sheet of stamps exactly as originally purchased at the post office.

Perforations. Rows of small, usually round holes, placed between the stamps on a sheet so that they can easily be separated. If a stamp has perforations on only one, two or three sides instead of on all four sides, it is known as a *part-perforate*.

Philately. The official, formal word for stamp collecting. Similarly, a stamp collector is called a *philatelist*.

Postage due. A stamp put on a letter or package at the post office when the sender has used insufficient postage. This stamp indicates the amount of money that must be collected by the postman from the person who receives the mail.

Regular issue. The everyday, ordinary kind of stamp, as opposed to an airmail, special delivery, postage due, commemorative or other kind of special purpose stamp.

Watermark. A design or pattern incorporated into the paper upon which postage stamps are printed. Watermarks help to prevent forgeries.

Stamp Identifier Table and Index

This alphabetical list contains the names of all the countries in their own languages as well as in English. It also contains other words found on stamps that will help you identify them. The numbers refer to the small boldface numerals that appear just above and to the left of the names of the countries in the album (see "Using This Album," page iv).

UNITED STATES OF AMERICA

North America. *Area:* 3,717810 sq. mi. (the fourth largest country in the world). *Pop.:* 294,043,000. *Cap.:* Washington, D.C. *Lang.:* English. *Money:* 100 cents = 1 dollar.

1883		1890–93			1890–93		
	1890–93						
			1890–93				
	1893						
1902–3		1902–3		1902–3			
1917–19	1917–19	1917–19	1917–19	1917–19			1917–19
1922–34	1922–34	1922–34		1922–34			

1927

1929

1929

1930

1932

1932

1932

1933

1933

1933

1933

1934

1934

1934

1934

1934

1935

1940

1936

1936

1936–7

1939

1940

1945

1938–54		1938–54		1938–54	1938–54	1938–54	
1938–54		1938–54		1938–54		1938–54	1938–54
1940	1940	1940	1940	1940	1940	
1940		1940				1940
1947		1948	1958	1960	1960	1960
1940	1940	1942	1942	1943	1943		1946
	1952					
1947			1956		1956

|  | | |  | | |
| 1943–44 | | | 1945–46 | | |

|  | | | | | |
| 1964–68 | 1964–68 | 1964–68 | 1964–68 | 1964–68 | 1964–68 |

| | | | | | |
| 1964–68 | 1964–68 | 1964–68 | 1964–68 | 1964–68 | 1964–68 |

|  | | | | |  |
| 1964–68 | 1964–68 | 1964–68 | 1964–68 | 1964–68 | 1966–73 |

| | | | | | |
| 1968 | 1968 | 1968–69 | 1968–69 | 1959 | 1959 |

| | | | | | |
| 1959 | 1959 | 1960 | 1960 | 1960 | 1960 |

| | | | | |
| 1960–61 | 1960–61 | 1960–61 | 1960–61 | |

|  |  |  | |  |  |
| 1962 | | 1964 | 1964 | 1966 | 1966 |

1960–66

1962–66

1966

1965–73

1965–73

1965–73

1965–73

1965–73

1965–73

1965–73

1965–73

1965–73

1965–73

1965–73

1965–73

1965–73

1966–73

1966–73

1966–73

1967

1970

1970–74

1970–74

1970–74

1970–74

1970–74

1970–74

1970–74

1969

1969

1971

1971

1975

1975

1969

1969

1973

1973

1976

1973

1974

1974

1974

1974

1974

1973–74

1973–74

1973–77

1975–77

1975–77

1975–77

1975–77

1975–77

1975–77

1975–77

1977

1977

1975

1975

1975

1975

1976

1976

1976

1976

1975

1976

1976

1977

	1978	1978	1978
1981–82		1986–94	

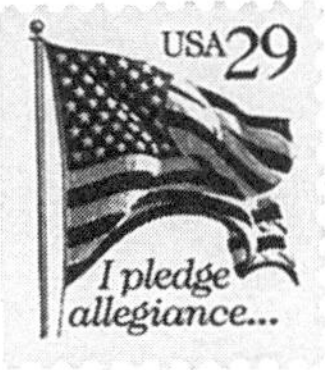

USA29
I pledge
allegiance...
1992–95

USA29
1992–95

33USA
1999

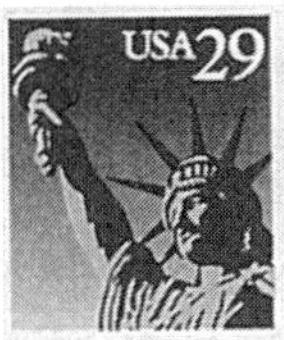

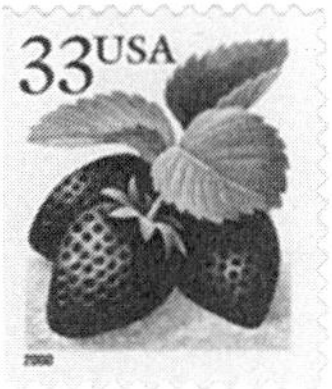

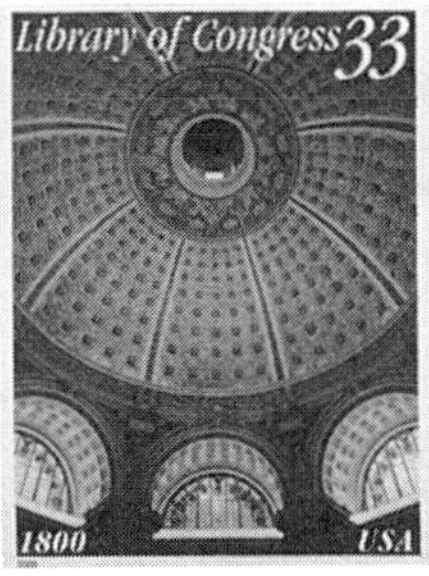

Library of Congress 33
1800
USA
2000

2002

2003

2003

2003

Airmails and Special Delivery

1941–44

1946

1957

1959

1959–60

1961

1988

1989

1991

2001

1944

1957

2

UNITED NATIONS

Association of sovereign states with membership open to all countries of the world which espouse the cause of peace. There are currently 191 nations represented at the U.N. The first United Nations stamps were issued in 1951.

1951

1966

1969

1974

3					
CANAL ZONE	Strip of land extending 5 miles on each side of the axis of the Panama Canal under jurisdiction		of the U.S. by treaty with Panama, 1903–1999. *Area:* 553 sq. mi. *Pop.:* 43,000.		

1924–26	1949	1958	

4		
HAWAII	Became the 50th state in 1959. Formerly a kingdom and republic, it issued its own stamps from 1851 to 1899.	

1882	1890–91	1899

5		
AFGHANISTAN	Central Asia. *Area:* 250,001 sq. mi. (slightly smaller than Texas). *Pop.:* 23,897,000. *Cap.:*	Kabul. *Langs.:* Pashtu and Persian. *Money:* 100 pouls = 1 rupee Afghani.

1931–38	1950

6		
ALBANIA [Shqiperia]	SE Europe. *Area:* 11,100 sq. mi. (slightly larger than Maryland). *Pop.:* 3,166,000. *Cap.:* Tirana.	*Langs.:* Albanian and Greek. *Money:* 100 quintar = 1 lek.

1920	1925

7		
ANDORRA [Andorre]	SW Europe. *Area:* 181 sq. mi. (half the size of New York City). *Pop.:* 69,150. *Cap.:* Andorra la Vella. *Langs.:* Catalan (off.), French and Spanish.	*Money:* 100 centimes = 1 franc (French currency) and 100 centimos = 1 peseta (Spanish currency).

1931	1944	1945

<table>
<tr><td>8</td></tr>
</table>

| **ARGENTINA** | South America. *Area:* 1,068,301 sq. mi. (four times the size of Texas). *Pop.:* 38,428,000. *Cap.:* | Buenos Aires. *Lang.:* Spanish. *Money:* 100 centavos = 1 peso. |

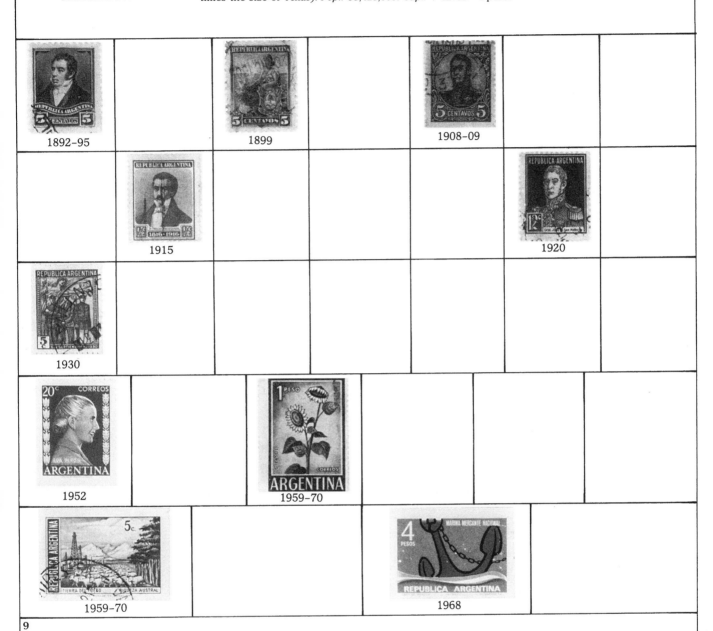

1892–95   1899   1908–09

1915   1920

1930

1952   1959–70

1959–70   1968

<table>
<tr><td>9</td></tr>
</table>

| **ALGERIA**
[Algérie] | N Africa. Formerly a semi-autonomous département of France. *Area:* 919,594 sq. mi. (more than three times the size of Texas). *Pop.:* 31,800,000. | *Cap.:* Algiers. *Langs.:* Arabic, Berber and French. *Money:* 100 centimes = 1 franc; since 1964, 100 centimes = 1 dinar. |

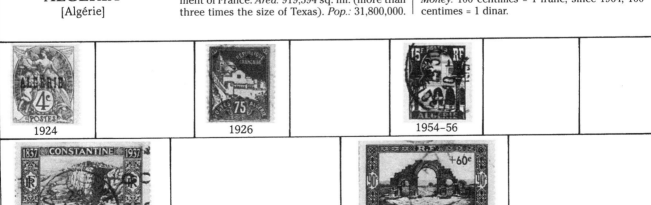

1924   1926   1954–56

1937   1942

AUSTRIA

[Österreich]

Central Europe. In 1867, the Austro-Hungarian Monarchy was established, with Austria and Hungary as equal partners. After World War I the various nationalities of the monarchy established their own states. *Area:* 32,376 sq. mi. (slightly smaller than Maine). *Pop.:* 8,116,000. *Cap.:* Vienna. *Langs.:* German and Slovene. *Money:* 100 Heller = 1 Krone; 1925–2002, 100-Groschen = 1 Schilling; since 2002, 100 cents = 1 Euro.

1867–72			1896		1906–07
	1908		1908		1908
1929		1930			1934
1946–47		1948–49		1951–52	
	1957–60	1957–60			1966
1925		1926			1926

BOSNIA and HERZEGOVINA

Located SE Europe. Provinces of Austria-Hungary from 1908 to 1918; of Yugoslavia from 1918 until independence in 1991.

1912–14

1917

1917

BELGIUM

[Belgique, België]

W Europe. *Area:* 11,780 sq. mi. (slightly larger than Maryland). *Pop.:* 10,318,000. *Cap.:* Brussels. *Off. Langs.:* Dutch, French, and German. *Money:*

100 centimes = 1 franc; 5 francs = 1 belga; since 2002, 100 cents = 1 Euro.

1869–70	1886–91
1905–07	1915
1919–20	
1921–23	1921–23
1929–30	1931
1938–42	1950
1950–52	1957–60
1958	1960
1961	1961

13

CONGO

[Congo Belge, République Démocratique du Congo, Zaire]

Central Africa. Former Belgian colony. *Area:* 905,567 sq. mi. (one-fourth the size of the United States). *Pop.:* 52,771,000. *Cap.:* Kinshasa. *Off.*

Lang.: French. *Money:* 100 makuta = 1 zaire; since 1998, 100 centimes = 1 franc.

1925–26

1925–26

1952–53

1965

1961

14

RUANDA-URUNDI

[Burundi, Rwanda]

E central Africa. Former Belgian colony. *Area:* 10,169 sq. mi. (the size of Maryland). *Pop.:* 8,387,000. *Cap.:* Kigali. *Langs.:* French, Kinyarwanda and Swahili. *Money:* 100 centimes = 1 franc.

1931

1966

1965

15

BOLIVIA

Central South America. *Area:* 424,162 sq. mi. (the size of Texas and California combined). *Pop.:* 8,808,000. *Caps.:* Sucre and La Paz. *Langs.:*

Spanish, Quechua and Aymara. *Money:* 100 centavos = 1 peso; since 1986, 100 centavos = 1 boliviano.

1931

1933

1939

1943

1946

1953

1962

1962

BRAZIL

[Brasil]

South America. *Area:* 3,286,486 sq. mi. (a little larger than the United States excluding Alaska and Hawaii). *Pop.:* 178,470,000. *Cap.:* Brasilia.

Lang.: Portuguese. *Money:* 1000 reis = 1 milreis; 100 centavos = 1 cruzeiro; since 1994, 100 centavos = 1 real.

1922–23

1929

1931–34

1941–42

1941–42

1954–56

1958

1958

1960

1963

1972–74

MYANMAR
[Burma]

SE Asia. Formerly part of British India. *Area:* 261,970 sq. mi. (nearly as large as Texas). *Pop.:* 49,485,000. *Cap.:* Rangoon. *Langs.:* Burmese and

English. *Money:* 12 pies = 1 anna; 15 annas = 1 rupee; since 1953, 100 pyas = 1 kyat.

1937

1938

1949

1964

CAMBODIA
[Cambodge, République Khmère, Democratic Kampuchea]

SE Asia. Former protectorate of France. *Area:* 69,900 sq. mi. (the size of Missouri). *Pop.:* 14,144,000. *Cap.:* Phnom Penh. *Langs.:* Khmer

and French. *Money:* 100 cents = 1 piaster; since 1955, 100 sen = 1 riel.

1959

1972

1972

BULGARIA

SW Europe. *Area:* 42,823 sq. mi. (slightly larger than Tennessee). *Pop.:* 7,897,000. *Cap.:* Sofia. | *Langs.:* Bulgarian, Turkish and Greek. *Money:* 100 stotinki = 1 lev.

1889		1896
1901–06	1911	1918–19
1930	1939	1946
1968	1968	

CHILE

SW South America. *Area:* 292,260 sq. mi. (larger than Texas). *Pop.:* 15,805,000. *Cap.:* Santiago. | *Lang.:* Spanish. *Money:* 100 centesimos = 1 escudo; since 1975, 1000 escudos = 1 peso.

1905–09	1929	1938–40
1956	1966	

ESTONIA
[Eesti]

Former Socialist republic of the Soviet Union, N Europe. As an independent republic, it issued its own stamps from 1918 to 1940. Regained sovereignty in 1991.

1922–24	1928–29	1936–39

22		

COLOMBIA

South America. *Area:* 439,735 sq. mi. (larger than Texas and California combined). *Pop.:* | 44,222,000. *Cap.:* Bogota. *Lang.:* Spanish. *Money:* 100 centavos = 1 peso.

1932

1936

1939

1945

1947

1956

1957

1968

23		

COSTA RICA

Central America. *Area:* 19,730 sq. mi. (slightly smaller than West Virginia). *Pop.:* 4,173,000. | *Cap.:* San Jose. *Lang.:* Spanish. *Money:* 100 centimos = 1 colon.

1937

1947

1952

1956

1959

24		

CUBA

West Indies. *Area:* 42,803 sq. mi. (nearly as large as Pennsylvania). *Pop.:* 11,300,000. *Cap.:* Havana. *Lang.:* Spanish. *Money:* 100 centavos = 1 peso.

1917–31

1936

1956

CHINA

[People's Republic of China
(mainland China)]

Central and E Asia. *Area:* 3,705,404 sq. mi. (slightly larger than the United States). *Pop.:* 1,304,196,000. *Cap.:* Beijing. *Lang.:* Mandarin. *Money:* 100 fen = 1 yuan.

1923

1931–37

1940

1941

1942–43

1946–47

1946

1947

1960

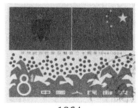
1964

CHINA

[Republic of China (Taiwan)]

Island of Formosa in South China Sea. Split from the mainland government in 1949. *Area:* 13,892 sq. mi. (the size of Maryland and Delaware combined). *Pop.:* 22,603,000. *Cap.:* Taipei. *Lang.:* Mandarin. *Money:* 100 cents = 1 dollar.

1953

1954

1956

1961

1972

1974

CZECHOSLOVAKIA

[Ceskoslovensko, Czech Republic]

Former nation, 1918 to 1939 and 1945 to 1993. Split with Slovakia to form the Czech Republic in 1993. *Area:* 30,450 sq. mi. *Pop.:* 10,236,000.

Cap.: Prague. *Off. Lang.:* Czech. *Money:* 100 halers = 1 koruna.

1918–19	1919–20	1920
1920	1920–25	1925
1930	1930	1936–37
1945	1945–46	1949
1952	1953	1957
1958	1968	

BOHEMIA and MORAVIA [Cechy a Moravia]   A German Protectorate from 1939 to 1945.

1942	1939–40	1943

SLOVAKIA   [Slovensko]   A nominally independent republic from 1939 to 1945.

1940–43	1943	1944

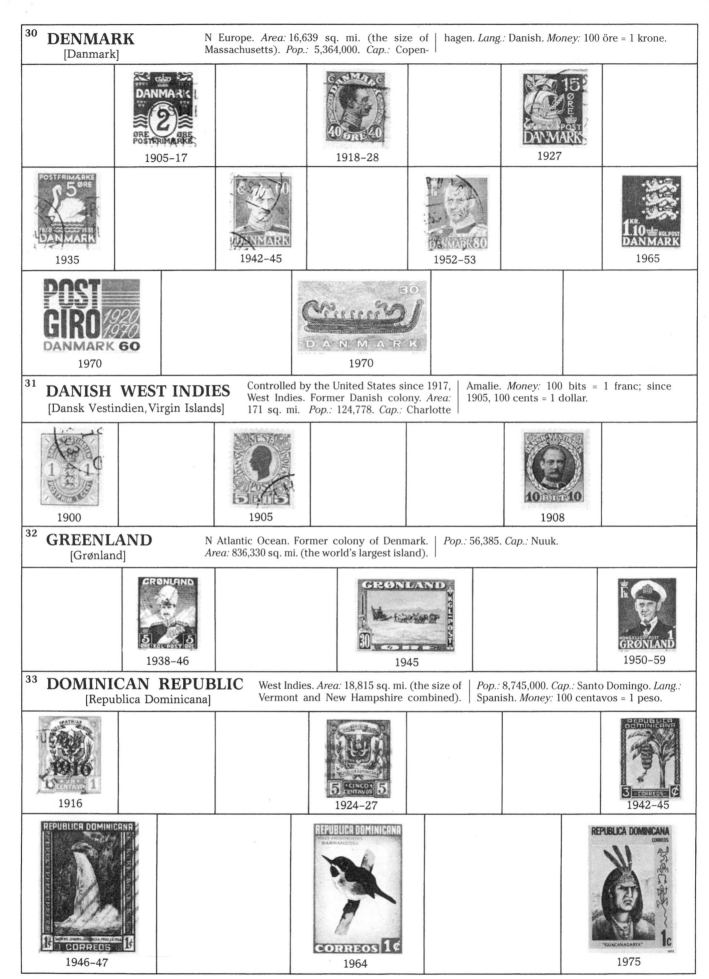

30 DENMARK
[Danmark]

N Europe. *Area:* 16,639 sq. mi. (the size of Massachusetts). *Pop.:* 5,364,000. *Cap.:* Copen- | hagen. *Lang.:* Danish. *Money:* 100 öre = 1 krone.

1905–17

1918–28

1927

1935

1942–45

1952–53

1965

1970

1970

31 DANISH WEST INDIES
[Dansk Vestindien, Virgin Islands]

Controlled by the United States since 1917, West Indies. Former Danish colony. *Area:* 171 sq. mi. *Pop.:* 124,778. *Cap.:* Charlotte | Amalie. *Money:* 100 bits = 1 franc; since 1905, 100 cents = 1 dollar.

1900

1905

1908

32 GREENLAND
[Grønland]

N Atlantic Ocean. Former colony of Denmark. | *Pop.:* 56,385. *Cap.:* Nuuk.
Area: 836,330 sq. mi. (the world's largest island).

1938–46

1945

1950–59

33 DOMINICAN REPUBLIC
[Republica Dominicana]

West Indies. *Area:* 18,815 sq. mi. (the size of Vermont and New Hampshire combined). | *Pop.:* 8,745,000. *Cap.:* Santo Domingo. *Lang.:* Spanish. *Money:* 100 centavos = 1 peso.

1916

1924–27

1942–45

1946–47

1964

1975

<table>
<tr><td>34</td></tr>
</table>

ECUADOR

NW South America. *Area:* 109,483 sq. mi. (the size of Colorado). *Pop.:* 13,003,000. *Cap.:* Quito. | *Lang.:* Spanish. *Money:* 100 centavos = 1 sucre; since 2000, 100 cents = 1 dollar.

1911–13

1920

1935

1943–45

1948

1956

1964

1965

<table>
<tr><td>35</td></tr>
</table>

EGYPT

[Égypte, United Arab Republic]

N Africa. *Area:* 386,662 sq. mi. (the size of Texas and New Mexico combined). *Pop.:* 71,931,000. *Cap.:* Cairo. *Lang.:* Arabic. *Money:* 40 paras = 1 | piastre; since 1888, 1000 milliemes = 100 piastres = 1 pound.

1914

1921–22

1923–24

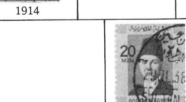
1937–44

1939–46

1944–46

1957

1946

1965

1965

ETHIOPIA

[Abyssinia, Éthiopie]

NE Africa. Formerly an empire. *Area:* 435,186 sq. mi. (about four-fifths the size of Alaska). *Pop.:* 70,678,000. *Cap.:* Addis Ababa. *Off. Lang.:*

Amharic. *Money:* 40 paras = 1 piastre; 1936–1986, 100 centimes = 1 taler; since 1986, 100 cents = 1 birr.

1928	1931	1942–44
1949–51		1969

FINLAND

[Suomi]

N Europe. *Area:* 130,128 sq. mi. (slightly smaller than Montana). *Pop.:* 5,207,000. *Cap.:* Helsinki. *Off. Langs.:* Finnish and Swedish. *Money:* 100

pennis = 1 markka; since 2002, 100 cents = 1 Euro.

1917–29	1925–29	1930
1937		1942
1957–58	1969	

HAITI

West Indies. *Area:* 10,714 sq. mi. (the size of Maryland). *Pop.:* 8,326,000. *Cap.:* Port-au-Prince.

Langs.: French and Créole. *Money:* 100 centimes = 1 gourde.

1933	1963	1974

FRANCE

W Europe. *Area:* 211,209 sq. mi. (four-fifths the size of Texas). *Pop.:* 60,144,000. *Cap.:* Paris. | *Lang.:* French. *Money:* 100 centimes = 1 franc; since 2002, 100 cents = 1 Euro.

1906–07

1923–26

1924–27

1930

1932

1936

1937

1938–39

1938–39

1941

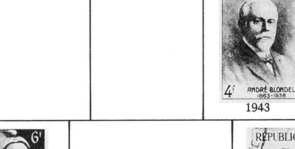
1943

1947

1951

1953

1957

1958

1961

1969

1970

1044 - DÉBARQUEMENT FRANÇAIS EN PROVENCE

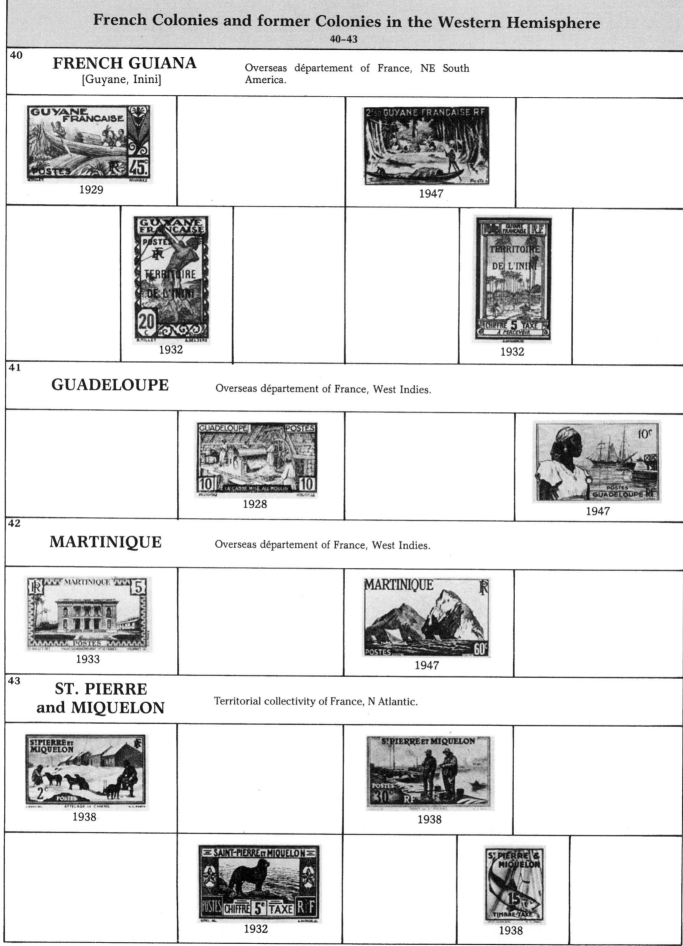

40

FRENCH GUIANA
[Guyane, Inini]

Overseas département of France, NE South America.

1929

1947

1932

1932

41

GUADELOUPE

Overseas département of France, West Indies.

1928

1947

42

MARTINIQUE

Overseas département of France, West Indies.

1933

1947

43

ST. PIERRE and MIQUELON

Territorial collectivity of France, N Atlantic.

1938

1938

1932

1938

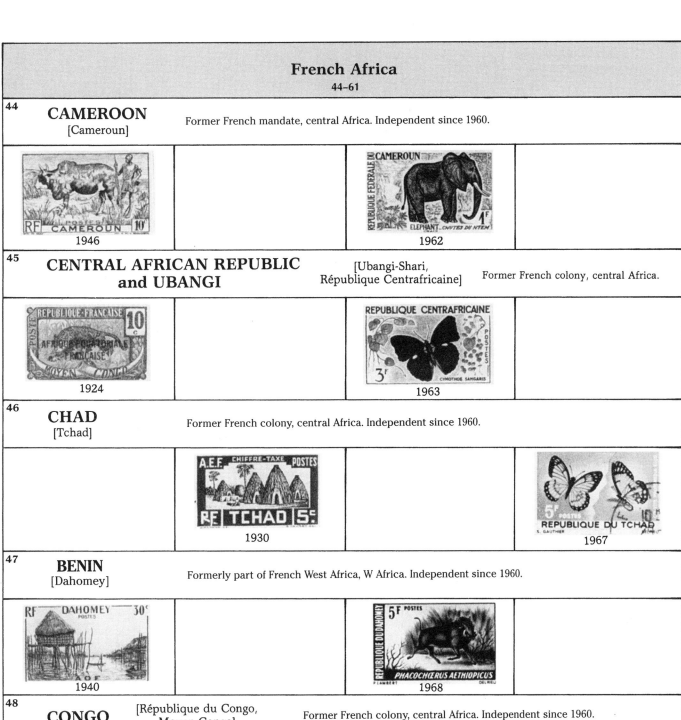

44

CAMEROON
[Cameroun]

Former French mandate, central Africa. Independent since 1960.

1946

1962

45

CENTRAL AFRICAN REPUBLIC and UBANGI

[Ubangi-Shari, République Centrafricaine]   Former French colony, central Africa.

1924

1963

46

CHAD
[Tchad]

Former French colony, central Africa. Independent since 1960.

1930

1967

47

BENIN
[Dahomey]

Formerly part of French West Africa, W Africa. Independent since 1960.

1940

1968

48

CONGO

[République du Congo, Moyen-Congo]   Former French colony, central Africa. Independent since 1960.

1933

1961

49

FRENCH EQUATORIAL AFRICA

[Afrique Équatoriale Française]   Former French colony, W Africa.

1937

1946

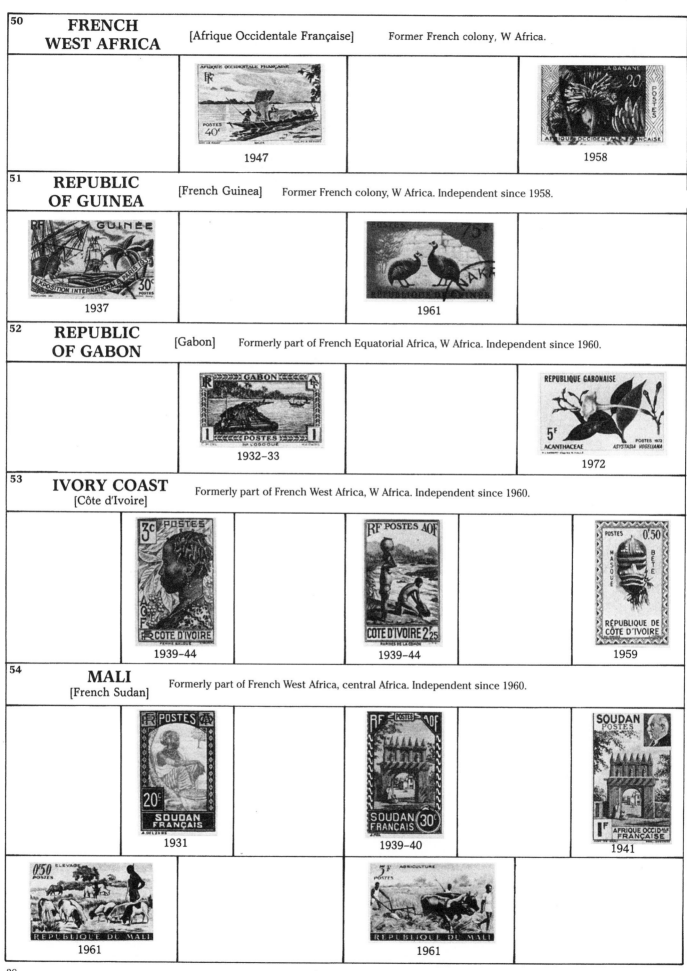

50 FRENCH WEST AFRICA [Afrique Occidentale Française]   Former French colony, W Africa.

1947

1958

51 REPUBLIC OF GUINEA [French Guinea]   Former French colony, W Africa. Independent since 1958.

1937

1961

52 REPUBLIC OF GABON [Gabon]   Formerly part of French Equatorial Africa, W Africa. Independent since 1960.

1932–33

1972

53 IVORY COAST [Côte d'Ivoire]   Formerly part of French West Africa, W Africa. Independent since 1960.

1939–44

1939–44

1959

54 MALI [French Sudan]   Formerly part of French West Africa, central Africa. Independent since 1960.

1931

1939–40

1941

1961

1961

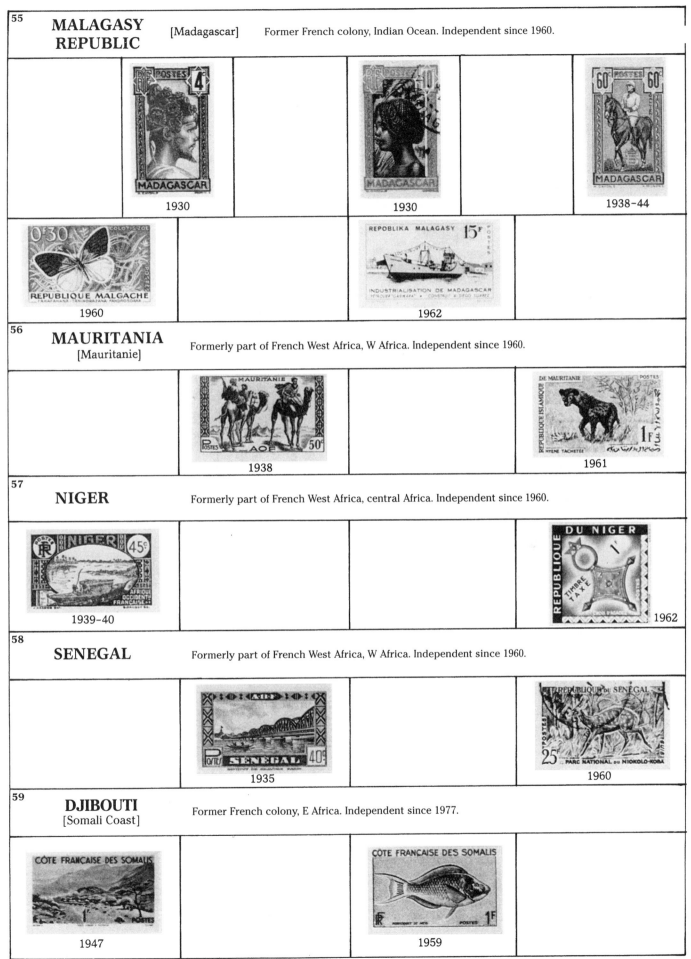

55 MALAGASY REPUBLIC　[Madagascar]　Former French colony, Indian Ocean. Independent since 1960.

1930

1930

1938–44

1960

1962

56 MAURITANIA
[Mauritanie]　Formerly part of French West Africa, W Africa. Independent since 1960.

1938

1961

57 NIGER　Formerly part of French West Africa, central Africa. Independent since 1960.

1939–40

1962

58 SENEGAL　Formerly part of French West Africa, W Africa. Independent since 1960.

1935

1960

59 DJIBOUTI
[Somali Coast]　Former French colony, E Africa. Independent since 1977.

1947

1959

60

TOGO

Formerly part of French West Africa, W Africa. Independent since 1960.

1940

1969

61

BURKINA FASO
[Haute Volta, Upper Volta]

Formerly part of French West Africa, W Africa. Independent since 1960; renamed Burkina Faso in 1984.

1928

1963

1966

French Asia and Oceania
62–68

62

FRENCH INDIA

[Établissements Français dans l'Inde]

Former French settlements, now part of India.

1942

1948

63

INDO-CHINA
[Indochine]

Former French colonies, SE Asia.

1907

1922–23

1931–32

1943–44

1943–44

1943–44

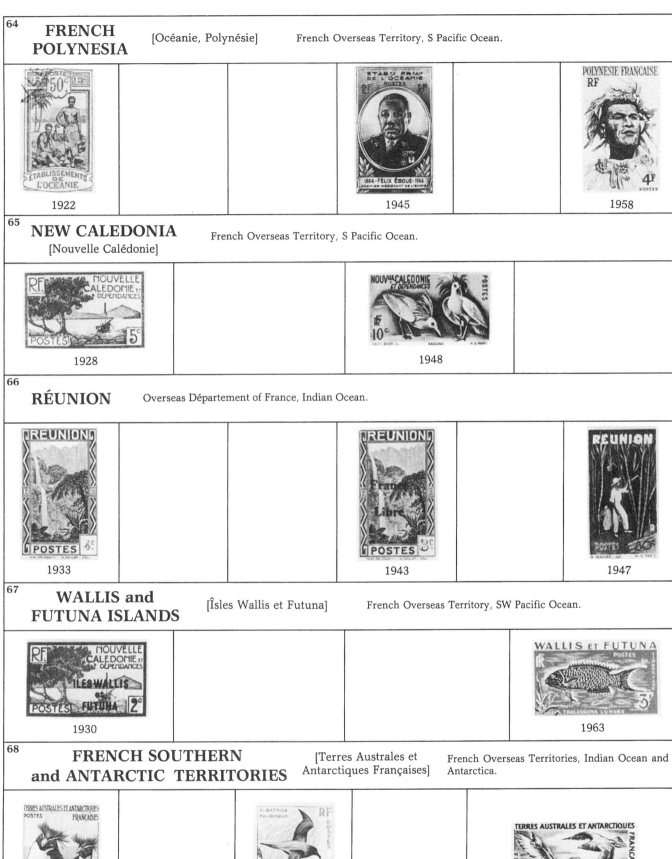

64

FRENCH POLYNESIA

[Océanie, Polynésie]   French Overseas Territory, S Pacific Ocean.

1922		1945		1958

65

NEW CALEDONIA
[Nouvelle Calédonie]

French Overseas Territory, S Pacific Ocean.

1928		1948	

66

RÉUNION

Overseas Département of France, Indian Ocean.

1933		1943	1947

67

WALLIS and FUTUNA ISLANDS

[Îsles Wallis et Futuna]   French Overseas Territory, SW Pacific Ocean.

1930		1963

68

FRENCH SOUTHERN and ANTARCTIC TERRITORIES

[Terres Australes et Antarctiques Françaises]   French Overseas Territories, Indian Ocean and Antarctica.

1956	1959	1959

GERMANY
[Deutsches Reich]

At the end of World War II in 1945, the Allies divided Germany into four zones. The three Western Zones were merged into the Federal Republic (West) and the Soviet Zone became the Democratic Republic (East). East and West reunited as a single German state in 1991.

1889–1900	1900	1916–19
1921–22	1921–23	1923 · 1923
1923	1923	1926
1928	1933–36	1936
1937	1938	1941–43

FEDERAL REPUBLIC OF GERMANY
[West Germany, Bundesrepublik Deutschland]

West Germany: 1945–1991.

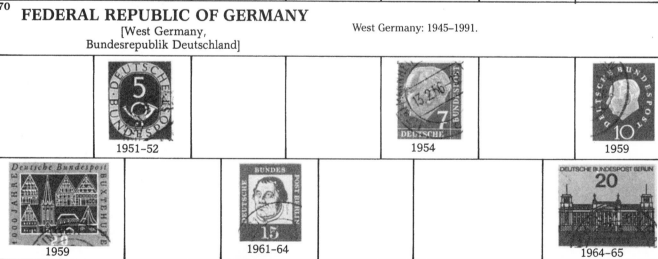

1951–52	1954	1959
1959	1961–64	1964–65

1970–73

1970–73

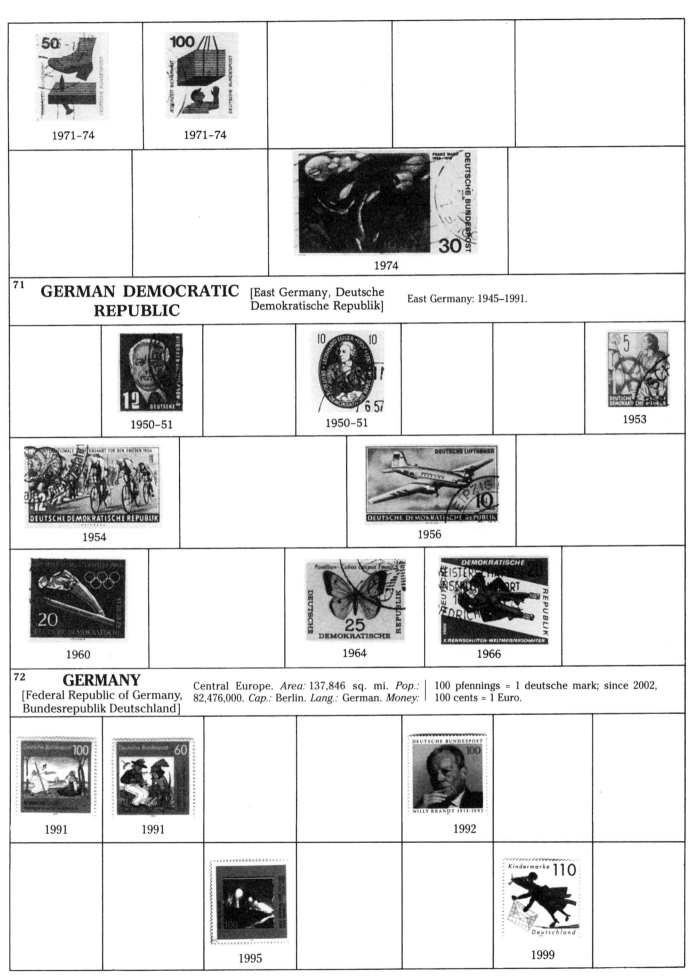

1971–74	1971–74			
		1974		

71 GERMAN DEMOCRATIC REPUBLIC

[East Germany, Deutsche Demokratische Republik]   East Germany: 1945–1991.

	1950–51	1950–51		1953
1954		1956		
1960		1964	1966	

72 GERMANY

[Federal Republic of Germany, Bundesrepublik Deutschland]

Central Europe. *Area:* 137,846 sq. mi. *Pop.:* 82,476,000. *Cap.:* Berlin. *Lang.:* German. *Money:* | 100 pfennings = 1 deutsche mark; since 2002, 100 cents = 1 Euro.

1991	1991		1992	
	1995		1999	

GREAT BRITAIN
[United Kingdom]

NW of the European Continent in the N Atlantic. *Area:* 94,525 sq. mi. (slightly smaller than Oregon). *Pop.:* 59,251,000. *Cap.:* London. *Lang.:* English. *Money:* 12 pence = 1 shilling; 20 shillings = 1 pound; since 1970, 100 pence = 1 pound.

1887–92	1900	1902	1912–13
	1922	1929	1934–36
1935		1936	1937–39
	1940		1946–47
1953		1952–55	
	1957	1960	
		1965	1969
	1971		

74

CANADA

Self-governing dominion in the British Commonwealth of Nations, North America. *Area:* 3,851,306 sq. mi. (larger than the United States). *Pop.:* 31,510,000. *Cap.:* Ottawa. *Off. Langs.:* English and French. *Money:* 100 cents = 1 dollar.

1902	1911–31	1927	1928–29
1932–33	1937–38	1937–38	1942–48
1942–48	1949–51	1953	
1954	1957		1962–64
1961–65	1967	1968	1973
1977	1978		

75

NEWFOUNDLAND

Former British Dominion, became the tenth province of the Dominion of Canada in 1949.

1911	1928	1937	

35

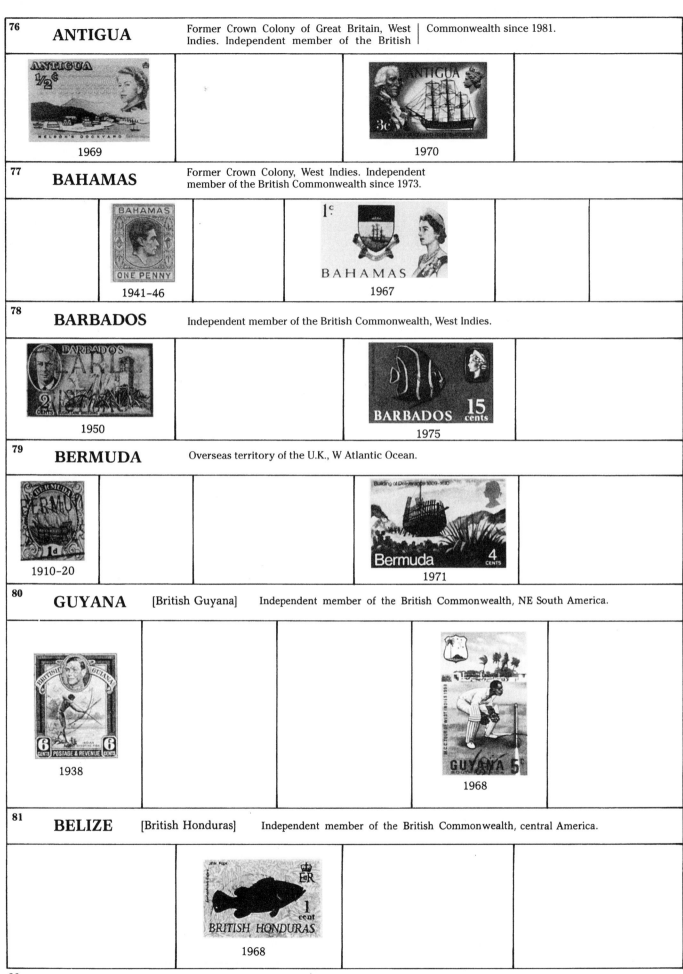

76 **ANTIGUA** Former Crown Colony of Great Britain, West | Commonwealth since 1981.
Indies. Independent member of the British |

1969

1970

77 **BAHAMAS** Former Crown Colony, West Indies. Independent
member of the British Commonwealth since 1973.

1941–46

1967

78 **BARBADOS** Independent member of the British Commonwealth, West Indies.

1950

1975

79 **BERMUDA** Overseas territory of the U.K., W Atlantic Ocean.

1910–20

1971

80 **GUYANA** [British Guyana] Independent member of the British Commonwealth, NE South America.

1938

1968

81 **BELIZE** [British Honduras] Independent member of the British Commonwealth, central America.

1968

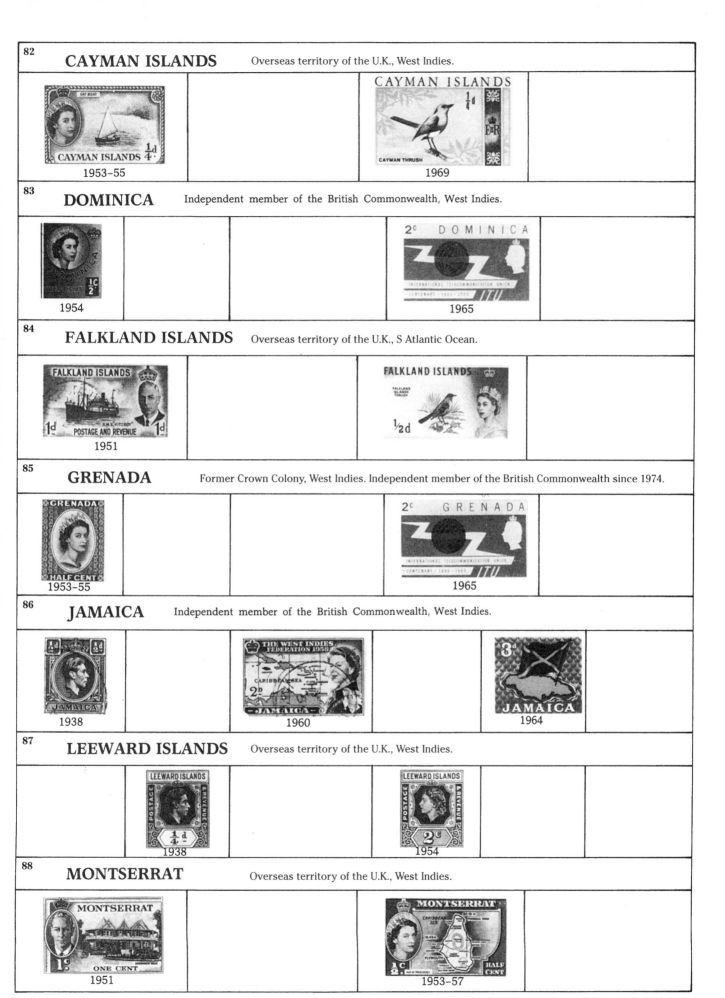

82

CAYMAN ISLANDS   Overseas territory of the U.K., West Indies.

1953–55

1969

83

DOMINICA   Independent member of the British Commonwealth, West Indies.

1954

1965

84

FALKLAND ISLANDS   Overseas territory of the U.K., S Atlantic Ocean.

1951

85

GRENADA   Former Crown Colony, West Indies. Independent member of the British Commonwealth since 1974.

1953–55

1965

86

JAMAICA   Independent member of the British Commonwealth, West Indies.

1938

1960

1964

87

LEEWARD ISLANDS   Overseas territory of the U.K., West Indies.

1938

1954

88

MONTSERRAT   Overseas territory of the U.K., West Indies.

1951

1953–57

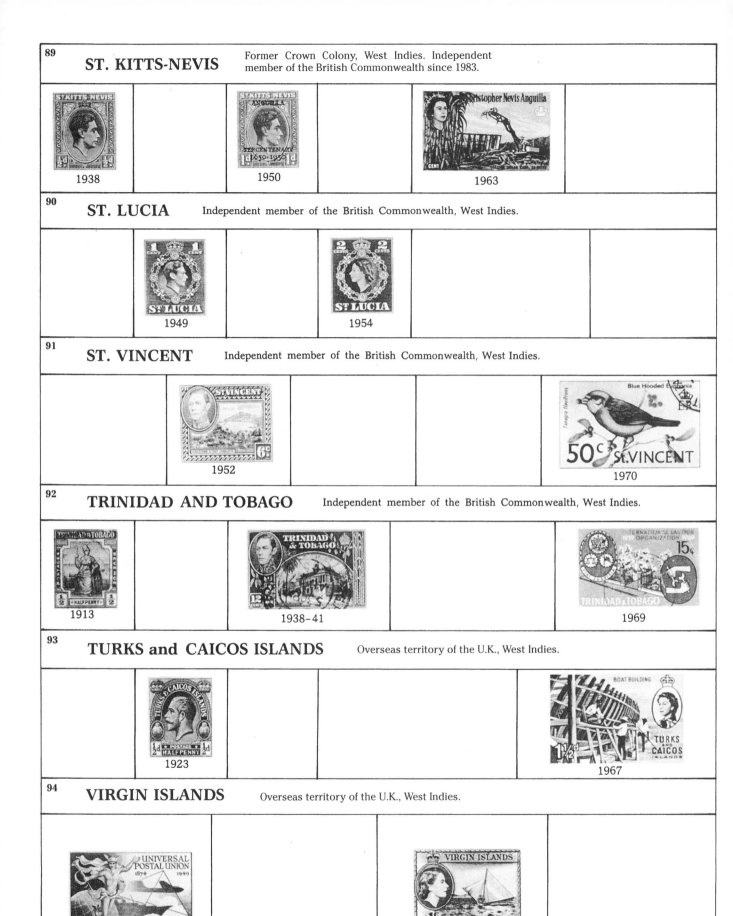

89

ST. KITTS-NEVIS
Former Crown Colony, West Indies. Independent member of the British Commonwealth since 1983.

1938   1950   1963

90

ST. LUCIA
Independent member of the British Commonwealth, West Indies.

1949   1954

91

ST. VINCENT
Independent member of the British Commonwealth, West Indies.

1952   1970

92

TRINIDAD AND TOBAGO
Independent member of the British Commonwealth, West Indies.

1913   1938–41   1969

93

TURKS and CAICOS ISLANDS
Overseas territory of the U.K., West Indies.

1923   1967

94

VIRGIN ISLANDS
Overseas territory of the U.K., West Indies.

1949   1956

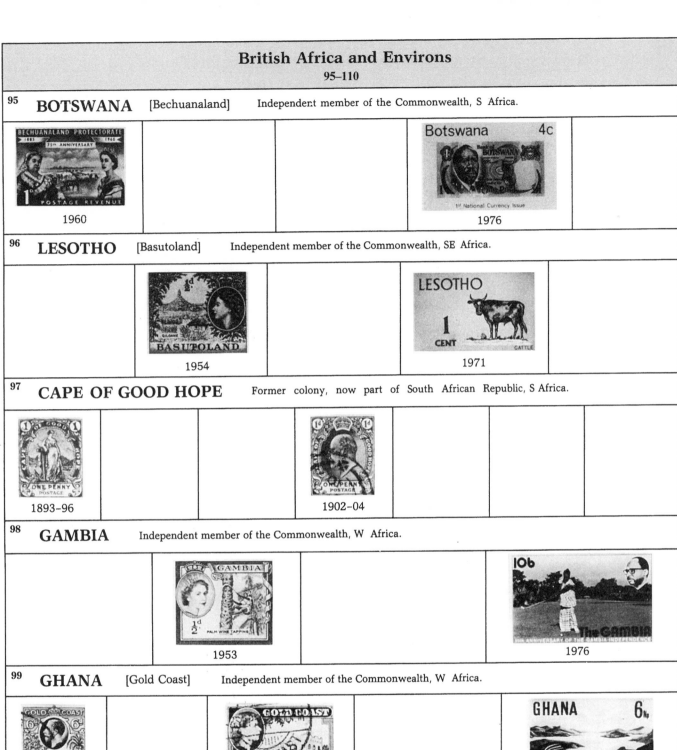

British Africa and Environs
95–110

95 BOTSWANA [Bechuanaland]   Independent member of the Commonwealth, S Africa.

1960		1976

96 LESOTHO [Basutoland]   Independent member of the Commonwealth, SE Africa.

	1954	1971

97 CAPE OF GOOD HOPE   Former colony, now part of South African Republic, S Africa.

1893–96	1902–04	

98 GAMBIA   Independent member of the Commonwealth, W Africa.

	1953	1976

99 GHANA [Gold Coast]   Independent member of the Commonwealth, W Africa.

1928	1952–54	1976

100 KENYA, UGANDA and TANZANIA [Tanganyika]   Independent members of the Commonwealth, E Africa.

1935	1953–59	1960–61	1963

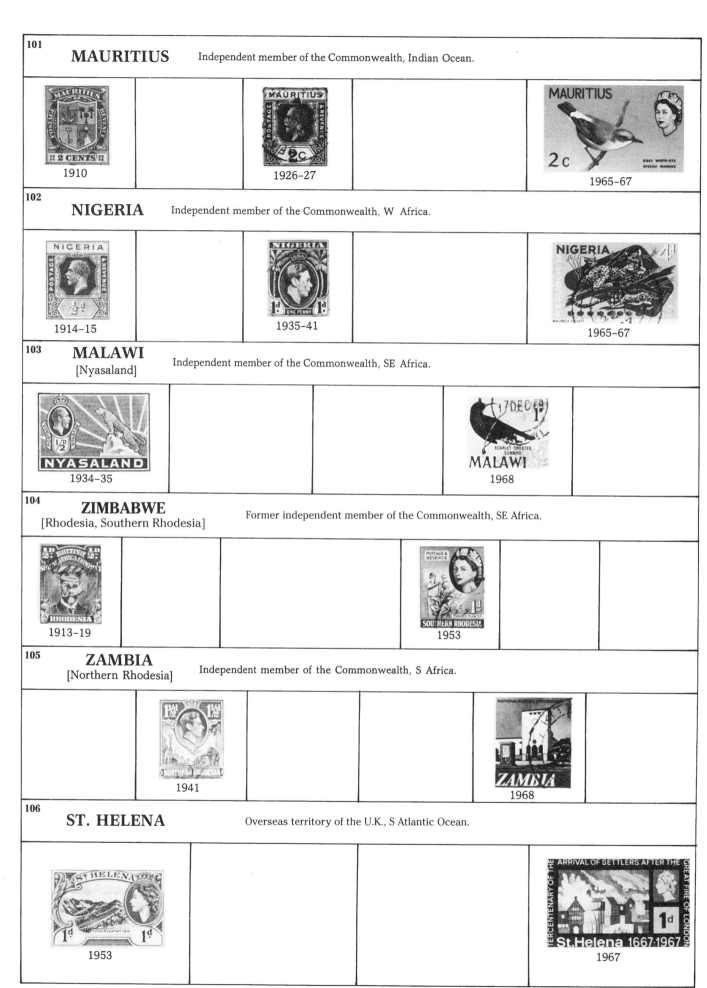

101

MAURITIUS
Independent member of the Commonwealth, Indian Ocean.

1910   1926–27   1965–67

102

NIGERIA
Independent member of the Commonwealth, W Africa.

1914–15   1935–41   1965–67

103

MALAWI
[Nyasaland]
Independent member of the Commonwealth, SE Africa.

1934–35   1968

104

ZIMBABWE
[Rhodesia, Southern Rhodesia]
Former independent member of the Commonwealth, SE Africa.

1913–19   1953

105

ZAMBIA
[Northern Rhodesia]
Independent member of the Commonwealth, S Africa.

1941   1968

106

ST. HELENA
Overseas territory of the U.K., S Atlantic Ocean.

1953   1967

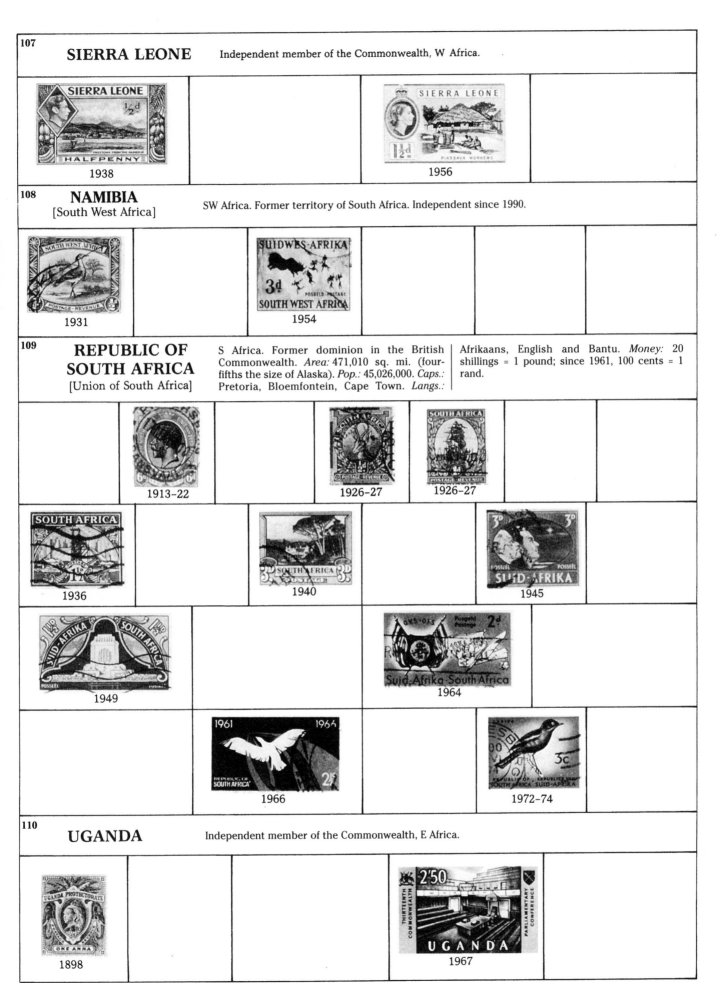

107

SIERRA LEONE   Independent member of the Commonwealth, W Africa.

1938

1956

108

NAMIBIA
[South West Africa]   SW Africa. Former territory of South Africa. Independent since 1990.

1931

1954

109

REPUBLIC OF SOUTH AFRICA
[Union of South Africa]

S Africa. Former dominion in the British Commonwealth. *Area:* 471,010 sq. mi. (four-fifths the size of Alaska). *Pop.:* 45,026,000. *Caps.:* Pretoria, Bloemfontein, Cape Town. *Langs.:*

Afrikaans, English and Bantu. *Money:* 20 shillings = 1 pound; since 1961, 100 cents = 1 rand.

1913–22

1926–27

1926–27

1936

1940

1945

1949

1964

1966

1972–74

110

UGANDA   Independent member of the Commonwealth, E Africa.

1898

1967

111

AUSTRALIA

Self-governing dominion in the British Commonwealth, E Indian Ocean, W Pacific Ocean. *Area:* 2,967,907 sq. mi. (almost as large as the United States excluding Alaska and Hawaii). *Pop.:* 19,731,000. *Cap.:* Canberra. *Lang.:* English. *Money:* 12 pence = 1 shilling; since 1966, 100 cents = 1 dollar.

	1913		1914–23		1935
	1937–38		1937–38		1942
	1947–48		1956–57		1959–60
	1965		1970		

112

CYPRUS

Independent member of the Commonwealth, Mediterranean Sea.

1924			1937	
1955		1962		1972

113

FIJI

Former Crown Colony, W South Pacific. Independent member of the British Commonwealth since 1970.

	1954–56		1956	

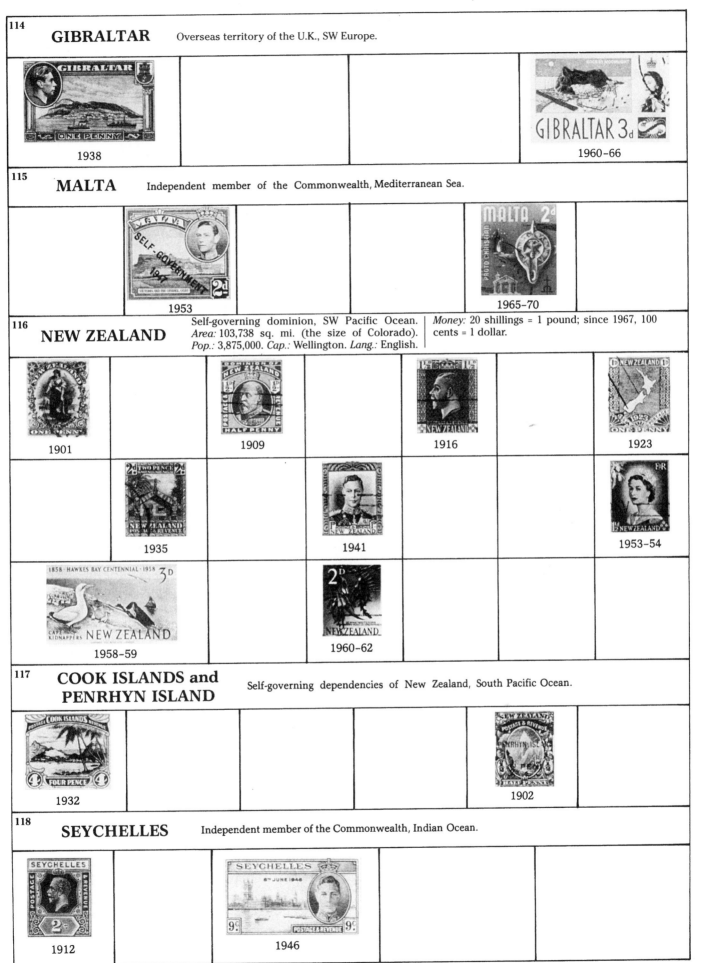

114

GIBRALTAR Overseas territory of the U.K., SW Europe.

1938

1960–66

115

MALTA Independent member of the Commonwealth, Mediterranean Sea.

1953

1965–70

116

NEW ZEALAND

Self-governing dominion, SW Pacific Ocean. *Area:* 103,738 sq. mi. (the size of Colorado). *Pop.:* 3,875,000. *Cap.:* Wellington. *Lang.:* English.

Money: 20 shillings = 1 pound; since 1967, 100 cents = 1 dollar.

1901

1909

1916

1923

1935

1941

1953–54

1958–59

1960–62

117

COOK ISLANDS and PENRHYN ISLAND

Self-governing dependencies of New Zealand, South Pacific Ocean.

1932

1902

118

SEYCHELLES Independent member of the Commonwealth, Indian Ocean.

1912

1946

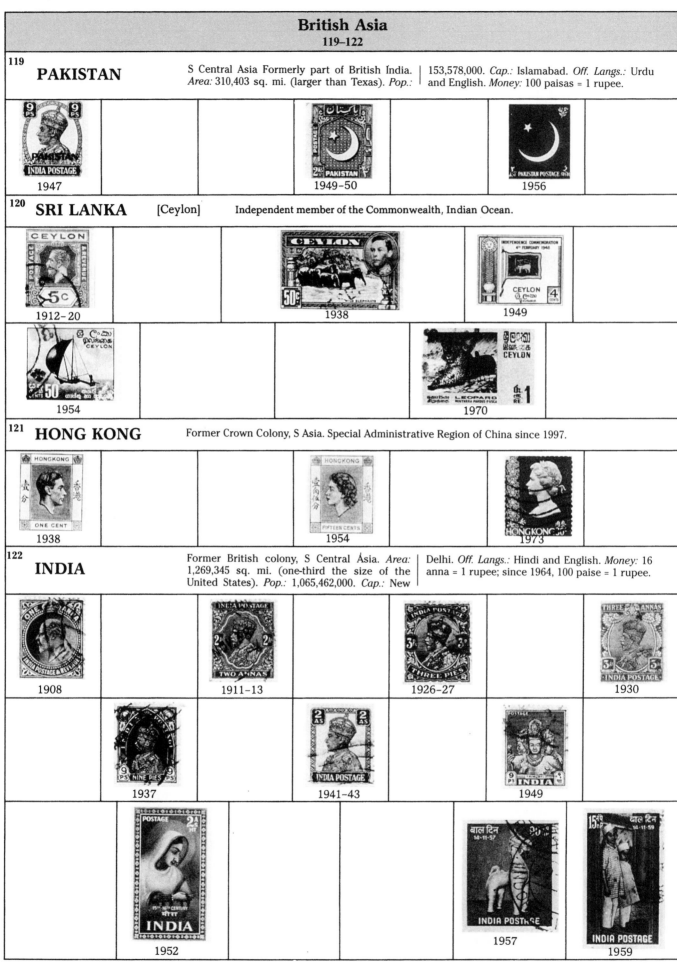

119 PAKISTAN — S Central Asia Formerly part of British India. *Area:* 310,403 sq. mi. (larger than Texas). *Pop.:* 153,578,000. *Cap.:* Islamabad. *Off. Langs.:* Urdu and English. *Money:* 100 paisas = 1 rupee.

| 1947 | | 1949–50 | 1956 |

120 SRI LANKA [Ceylon] — Independent member of the Commonwealth, Indian Ocean.

| 1912–20 | 1938 | 1949 |
| 1954 | 1970 | |

121 HONG KONG — Former Crown Colony, S Asia. Special Administrative Region of China since 1997.

| 1938 | 1954 | 1973 |

122 INDIA — Former British colony, S Central Asia. *Area:* 1,269,345 sq. mi. (one-third the size of the United States). *Pop.:* 1,065,462,000. *Cap.:* New Delhi. *Off. Langs.:* Hindi and English. *Money:* 16 anna = 1 rupee; since 1964, 100 paise = 1 rupee.

1908	1911–13	1926–27	1930
1937	1941–43	1949	
1952	1957	1959	

1965			1975–79	

INDIAN STATES

| Gwailor | | | | Jhind | |

1899		1942–48	1903–09	1913–14

| Patiala | | | Travancore | |

1932	1938–42	1939	

FEDERATION OF MALAYSIA, SINGAPORE, FEDERATED MALAY STATES, STRAITS SETTLEMENTS

Independent members of the Commonwealth, SE Asia.

	1922–32	1904–08	1950	
1951	1949	1938–40	1925	
1963	1965	1963–67	1962–67	

125		

GREECE   S Balkan Peninsula, SE Europe. *Area:* 50,942 sq. mi. (the size of New York State). *Pop.:* 10,976,000. *Cap.:* Athens. *Lang.:* Greek. *Money:*   100 lepta = 1 drachma; since 2002, 100 cents = 1 Euro.

1901		1911		1927	
1930		1937			1946
1949		1952		1956	
1959		1977			

126

GUATEMALA   Central America. *Area:* 42,042 sq. mi. (the size of Tennessee). *Pop.:* 12,347,000. *Cap.:* Guatemala   City. *Langs.:* Spanish and Maya-Quiche dialects. *Money:* 100 centavos = 1 quetzal.

1935		1946		1952	
1954		1966–67		1967	

46

| 127 **HONDURAS** | Central America. *Area:* 43,277 sq. mi. (slightly larger than Tennessee). *Pop.:* 6,941,000. Cap.: | Tegucigalpa. *Langs.:* Spanish and English. *Money:* 100 centavos = 1 lempira. |

1952   1966

| 128 **ICELAND** [Island] | N Atlantic Ocean. *Area:* 39,702 sq. mi. (the size of Virginia). *Pop.:* 290,000. Cap.: Reykjavik. *Lang.:* Icelandic. *Money:* 100 aurar = 1 krona. |

1939–45   1961   1972

| 129 **IRAQ** | W Asia. *Area:* 168,754 sq. mi. (slightly larger than California). *Pop.:* 25,175,000. Cap.: | Baghdad. *Langs:* Arabic and Kurdish. *Money:* 1000 fils = 1 dinar. |

1934   1941–42   1967

| 130 **IRELAND** [Eire] | E Atlantic Ocean. *Area:* 27,135 sq. mi. (the size of West Virginia). *Pop.:* 3,956,000. Cap.: Dublin. *Langs.:* English and Gaelic. *Money:* 12 pence = 1 | shilling; 1971–2002, 100 pence = 1 pound; since 2002, 100 cents = 1 Euro. |

1922–23   1931   1941   1943

1963   1969

| 131 **JORDAN** [Transjordan, Hashemite Kingdom of Jordan] | W Asia. *Area:* 35,637 sq. mi. (slightly smaller than Indiana). *Pop.:* 5,473,000. *Cap.:* Amman. | *Lang.:* Arabic. *Money:* 10 milliemes = 1 piastre; since 1951, 1000 fils = 1 Jordan dinar. |

1930

1954

1967

132

HUNGARY
[Magyarorzag]

SE Europe. Part of the Austro-Hungarian Empire until 1918. *Area:* 35,919 sq. mi. (slightly smaller than Indiana). *Pop.:* 9,877,000. *Cap.:* Budapest.

Lang.: Hungarian. *Money:* 100 fillar = 1 korona; after 1926, 100 fillar = 1 pengo; since 1946, 100 fillér = 1 forint.

1904–08	1916	1919	1926–27
	1932	1939	1943–45
1945–46		1946	1946–47
1959	1962		

133

ISRAEL

W Asia. *Area:* 8,019 sq. mi. (the size of Massachusetts). *Pop.:* 6,433,000. *Cap.:* Jerusalem. *Langs.:* Hebrew, Arabic and various

European languages. *Money:* 1000 mils = 1 Israeli pound; 1960–1980, 100 agorot = 1 Israeli pound; since 1980, 100 agorot = 1 shekel.

1948	1951		1953–56
1955–56	1957		1959
1964	1965	1971	

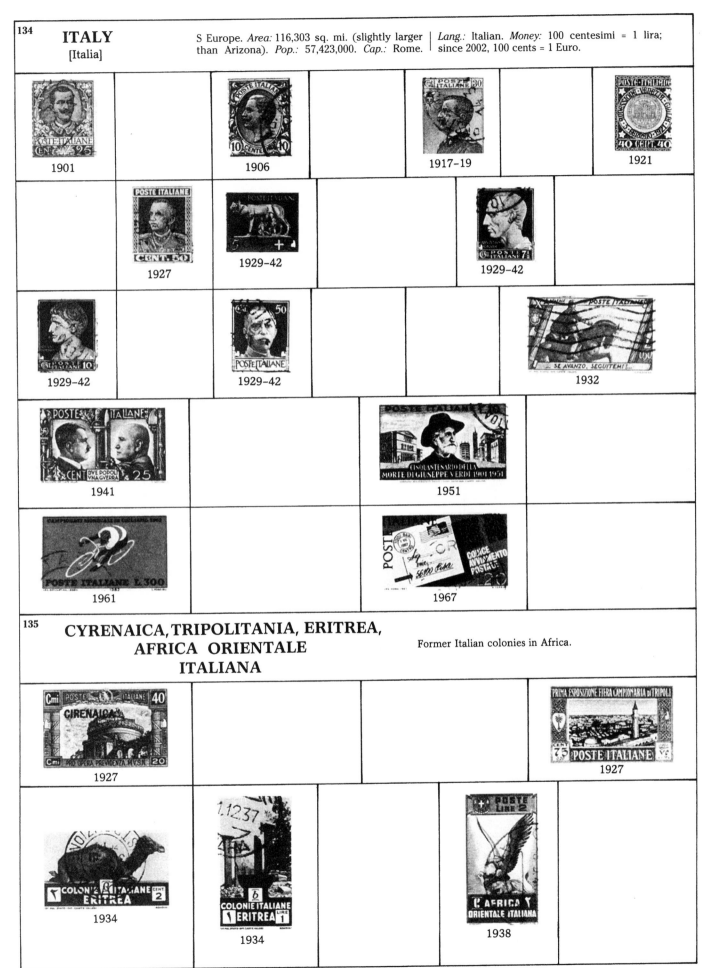

134   **ITALY**
     [Italia]

S Europe. *Area:* 116,303 sq. mi. (slightly larger than Arizona). *Pop.:* 57,423,000. *Cap.:* Rome. | *Lang.:* Italian. *Money:* 100 centesimi = 1 lira; since 2002, 100 cents = 1 Euro.

1901

1906

1917–19

1921

1927

1929–42

1929–42

1929–42

1929–42

1932

1941

1951

1961

1967

135   **CYRENAICA, TRIPOLITANIA, ERITREA, AFRICA ORIENTALE ITALIANA**

Former Italian colonies in Africa.

1927

1927

1934

1934

1938

136 IRAN
[Persia]

W Asia. *Area:* 636,296 sq. mi. (nearly two and one-half times the size of Texas). *Pop.:* 68,920,000. *Cap.:* Tehran. *Langs.:* Persian, Turkish, Kurdish and Arabic. *Money:* 100 dinar = 1 rial.

1894	1898	1904
1911	1915	1918
1926	1931–32	1933–39
1938–39	1944–46	
1962	1965	

137 JAPAN

NW Pacific Ocean. *Area:* 145,883 sq. mi. (slightly smaller than Montana). *Pop.:* 127,654,000. *Cap.:* Tokyo. *Lang.:* Japanese. *Money:* 100 sen = 1 yen.

1899–1910	1913–25	1921–23	1924–37
	1934–36	1936–38	1937–40

1941–45

1942–46

1946–49

1950–52

1955–56

1960–61

1966–67

1971–73

138 **RYUKYU ISLANDS**   Chain of islands belonging to Japan, E China Sea.

1948–51

1948–51

1958–59

139 **JUGOSLAVIA**
[Yugoslavia, Jugoslavija]

SE Europe. *Area:* 98,766 sq. mi. *Pop.:* 22,174,000. *Cap.:* Belgrade. *Langs.:* Serbo-Croatian, Macedonian and Slovene. *Money:* 100 paras = 1 dinar. Dissolved in 1991.

1921

1931–32

1939–40

1945

1953

1954

1961

1967

1974

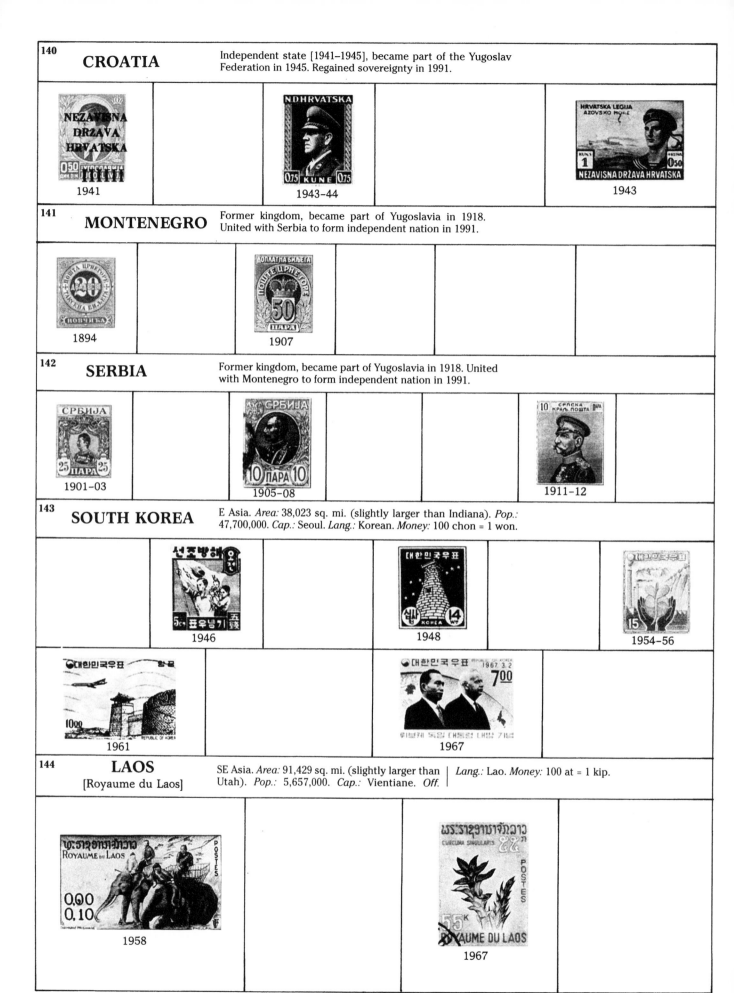

140 CROATIA

Independent state [1941–1945], became part of the Yugoslav Federation in 1945. Regained sovereignty in 1991.

1941

1943–44

1943

141 MONTENEGRO

Former kingdom, became part of Yugoslavia in 1918. United with Serbia to form independent nation in 1991.

1894

1907

142 SERBIA

Former kingdom, became part of Yugoslavia in 1918. United with Montenegro to form independent nation in 1991.

1901–03

1905–08

1911–12

143 SOUTH KOREA

E Asia. *Area:* 38,023 sq. mi. (slightly larger than Indiana). *Pop.:* 47,700,000. *Cap.:* Seoul. *Lang.:* Korean. *Money:* 100 chon = 1 won.

1946

1948

1954–56

1961

1967

144 LAOS
[Royaume du Laos]

SE Asia. *Area:* 91,429 sq. mi. (slightly larger than Utah). *Pop.:* 5,657,000. *Cap.:* Vientiane. *Off.* *Lang.:* Lao. *Money:* 100 at = 1 kip.

1958

1967

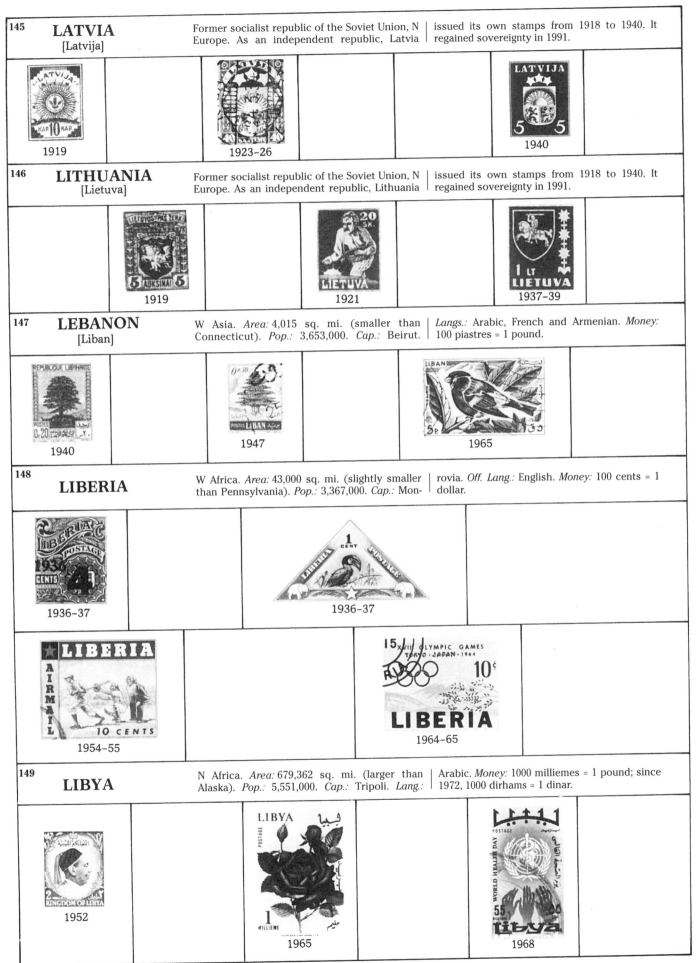

145	**LATVIA** [Latvija]	Former socialist republic of the Soviet Union, N Europe. As an independent republic, Latvia	issued its own stamps from 1918 to 1940. It regained sovereignty in 1991.	

145 · 1919 · 1923–26 · 1940

146	**LITHUANIA** [Lietuva]	Former socialist republic of the Soviet Union, N Europe. As an independent republic, Lithuania	issued its own stamps from 1918 to 1940. It regained sovereignty in 1991.	

146 · 1919 · 1921 · 1937–39

147	**LEBANON** [Liban]	W Asia. *Area:* 4,015 sq. mi. (smaller than Connecticut). *Pop.:* 3,653,000. *Cap.:* Beirut.	*Langs.:* Arabic, French and Armenian. *Money:* 100 piastres = 1 pound.	

147 · 1940 · 1947 · 1965

148	**LIBERIA**	W Africa. *Area:* 43,000 sq. mi. (slightly smaller than Pennsylvania). *Pop.:* 3,367,000. *Cap.:* Mon-	rovia. *Off. Lang.:* English. *Money:* 100 cents = 1 dollar.	

148 · 1936–37 · 1936–37 · 1954–55 · 1964–65

149	**LIBYA**	N Africa. *Area:* 679,362 sq. mi. (larger than Alaska). *Pop.:* 5,551,000. *Cap.:* Tripoli. *Lang.:*	Arabic. *Money:* 1000 milliemes = 1 pound; since 1972, 1000 dirhams = 1 dinar.	

149 · 1952 · 1965 · 1968

150 **LIECHTENSTEIN**	Central Europe. *Area:* 62 sq. mi. (the size of Washington, D.C.). *Pop.:* 33,000. *Cap.:* Vaduz. *Lang.:* German. *Money:* 100 rappen = 1 franc.	

1943

1954

1968

151 **LUXEMBOURG**	W Europe. *Area:* 999 sq. mi. (smaller than Rhode Island). *Pop.:* 453,000. *Cap.:* Luxembourg. *Langs.:* French, German and Luxembourgish. *Money:* 100	centimes = 1 frank; since 2002, 100 cents = 1 Euro.

1944–46

1951–53

1960–64

152 **MANCHURIA** [Manchukuo]	Region of the People's Republic of China. Former independent state under Japanese influence (1932 to 1945), NE Asia.

1936–37

1937–42

1942–45

1942–45

153 **MONACO**	S Europe. *Area:* 600 acres. *Pop.:* 32,000. *Cap.:* Monaco. *Langs.:* French, Monégasque, Italian	and English. *Money:* 100 sentimes = 1 franc; since 2002, 100 cents = 1 Euro.

1926–33

1937–39

1941–46

1952

1956

1962

154 **MONGOLIA**	Central Asia. *Area:* 604,247 sq. mi. (more than twice the size of Texas). *Pop.:* 2,594,000. *Cap.:*	Ulan Bator. *Langs.:* Mongolian and Turkic. *Money:* 100 mungo = 1 Tugrik.

1932

1932

1958

155					

MEXICO

Central America. *Area:* 761,601 sq. mi. (three times the size of Texas). *Pop.:* 103,457,000. *Cap.:* Mexico City. *Lang.:* Spanish. *Money:* 100 centimes = 1 peso.

1915		1917		1923	
1934		1940			1945
	1952		1954		1956–63
1962			1976		

156

MOROCCO
[Royaume du Maroc]

N Africa. *Area:* 172,414 sq. mi. (larger than California). *Pop.:* 30,566,000. *Cap.:* Rabat. *Langs.:* Arabic, Berber and French. *Money:* 100 centimes = 1 franc; since 1959, 100 centimes = 1 dirham.

1949	1955	1962	

157

NETHERLANDS
[Nederland]

NW Europe. *Area:* 16,033 sq. mi. (the size of Massachusetts, Connecticut and Rhode Island combined). *Pop.:* 16,149,000. *Caps.:* Amsterdam and The Hague. *Lang.:* Dutch. *Money:* 100 cents = 1 guilder or florin; since 2002, 100 cents = 1 Euro.

1899	1901–1910	1923	1924–26
	1926–27	1937	1940

 1943–44		1947–48		 1952
 1962		 1964		

158 NEDERLANDS ANTILLES

[Curacao, Aruba, Bonaire]

Former Dutch colony, integral part of the Kingdom of the Netherlands, West Indies.

1936		1941–42		 1965

159 SURINAME

[Dutch Guiana]

Former Dutch colony, integral part of the Kingdom of the Netherlands. NE South America.

1936		1948	1950	

160 DUTCH EAST INDIES

[Indonesia]   Former Dutch colony, W Pacific Ocean.

1912–40		1933–34	 1938

161 INDONESIA

[United States of Indonesia]

Formerly the Dutch East Indies. *Area:* 741,099 sq. mi. (larger than the state of Alaska). *Pop.:* 219,833,000. | *Cap.:* Jakarta. *Langs.:* Bahasa Indonesian and Javanese. *Money:* 100 sen = 1 rupiah.

 1953		 1962	 1969

162				

NICARAGUA

Central America. *Area:* 49,998 sq. mi. (slightly larger than Wisconsin). *Pop.:* 5,466,000. *Cap.:* | Managua. *Langs.:* Spanish and English. *Money:* 100 centavos = 1 cordoba.

1914

1927

1938

1949

1967

163				

NORWAY

[Norge]

N Europe. *Area:* 125,181 sq. mi. (slightly larger than New Mexico). *Pop.:* 4,533,000. *Cap.:* Oslo. | *Langs.:* Norwegian and Lapp. *Money:* 100 ore = 1 krone.

1926–34

1932

1940

1947

1957

1969

164				

PANAMA

Central America. *Area:* 30,193 sq. mi. (slightly larger than West Virginia). *Pop.:* 3,120,000. *Cap.:* | Panama City. *Langs.:* Spanish and English. *Money:* 100 centesimos = 1 balboa.

1924

1955

1962

165				

PARAGUAY

Central South America. *Area:* 157,047 sq. mi. (the state of California). *Pop.:* 5,878,000. *Cap.:* Asuncion. *Langs.:* Spanish and Guarani. *Money:* | 100 centavos = 1 peso; since 1944, 100 centimos = 1 guarani.

1942

1960

1961

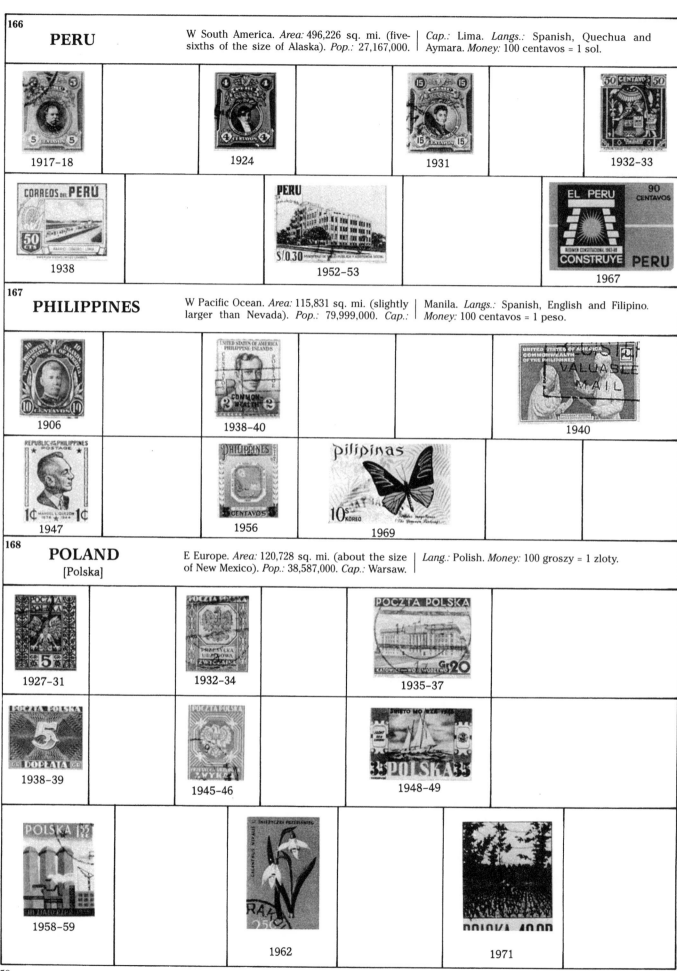

166

PERU

W South America. *Area:* 496,226 sq. mi. (five-sixths of the size of Alaska). *Pop.:* 27,167,000. | *Cap.:* Lima. *Langs.:* Spanish, Quechua and Aymara. *Money:* 100 centavos = 1 sol.

1917–18

1924

1931

1932–33

1938

1952–53

1967

167

PHILIPPINES

W Pacific Ocean. *Area:* 115,831 sq. mi. (slightly larger than Nevada). *Pop.:* 79,999,000. *Cap.:* | Manila. *Langs.:* Spanish, English and Filipino. *Money:* 100 centavos = 1 peso.

1906

1938–40

1940

1947

1956

1969

168

POLAND
[Polska]

E Europe. *Area:* 120,728 sq. mi. (about the size of New Mexico). *Pop.:* 38,587,000. *Cap.:* Warsaw. | *Lang.:* Polish. *Money:* 100 groszy = 1 zloty.

1927–31

1932–34

1935–37

1938–39

1945–46

1948–49

1958–59

1962

1971

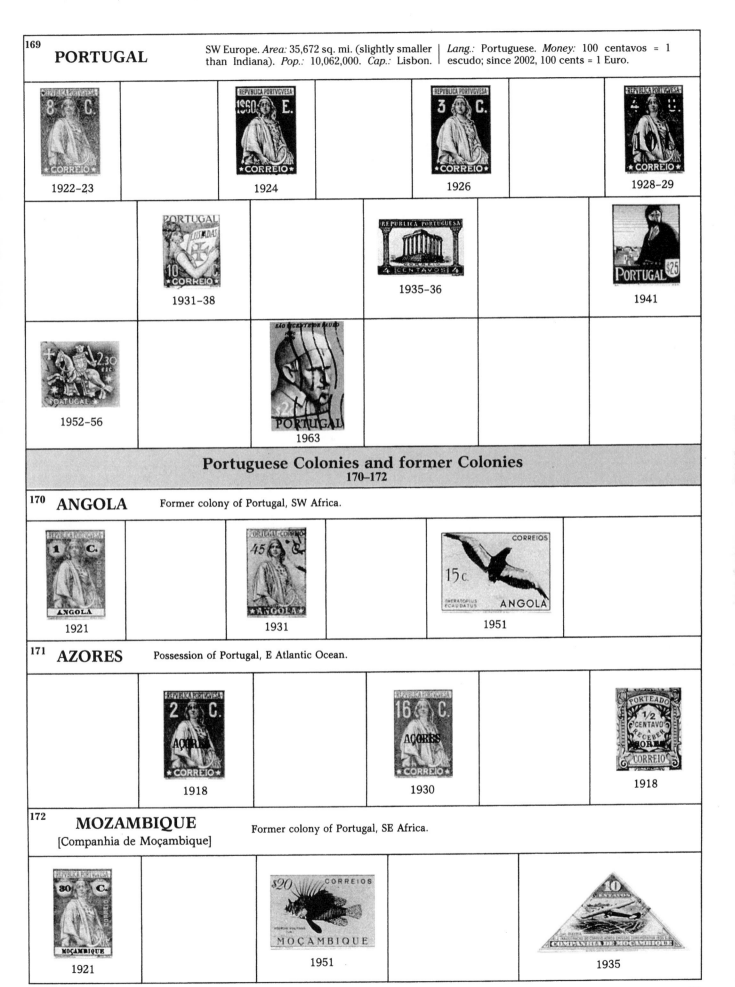

169

PORTUGAL

SW Europe. *Area:* 35,672 sq. mi. (slightly smaller than Indiana). *Pop.:* 10,062,000. *Cap.:* Lisbon. | *Lang.:* Portuguese. *Money:* 100 centavos = 1 escudo; since 2002, 100 cents = 1 Euro.

1922–23	1924	1926	1928–29
	1931–38	1935–36	1941
1952–56	1963		

Portuguese Colonies and former Colonies
170–172

170 ANGOLA   Former colony of Portugal, SW Africa.

1921	1931	1951

171 AZORES   Possession of Portugal, E Atlantic Ocean.

1918	1930	1918

172 MOZAMBIQUE
[Companhia de Moçambique]   Former colony of Portugal, SE Africa.

1921	1951	1935

173 **ROMANIA** SE Europe. *Area:* 91,699 sq. mi. (slightly smaller than Oregon). *Pop.:* 22,334,000. *Cap.:* Bucharest. | *Langs.:* Romanian and Hugarian. *Money:* 100 bani = 1 leu.

1928–29

1930–31

1940–42

1946

1950

1955–56

1957

1965

1965

174 **RUSSIA** [Union of Soviet Socialist Republics] Former socialist republic of the Soviet Union, 1917–1991. E Europe and N Asia. *Area:* 6,592,767 | sq. mi. *Pop.:* 143,246,000. *Cap.:* Moscow. *Off. Lang.:* Russian. *Money:* 100 kopecks = 1 ruble.

1902–06

1909–12

1917

1919

1922–23

1925–26

1929–31

1935

1941

1943–46

1947

1958

1973

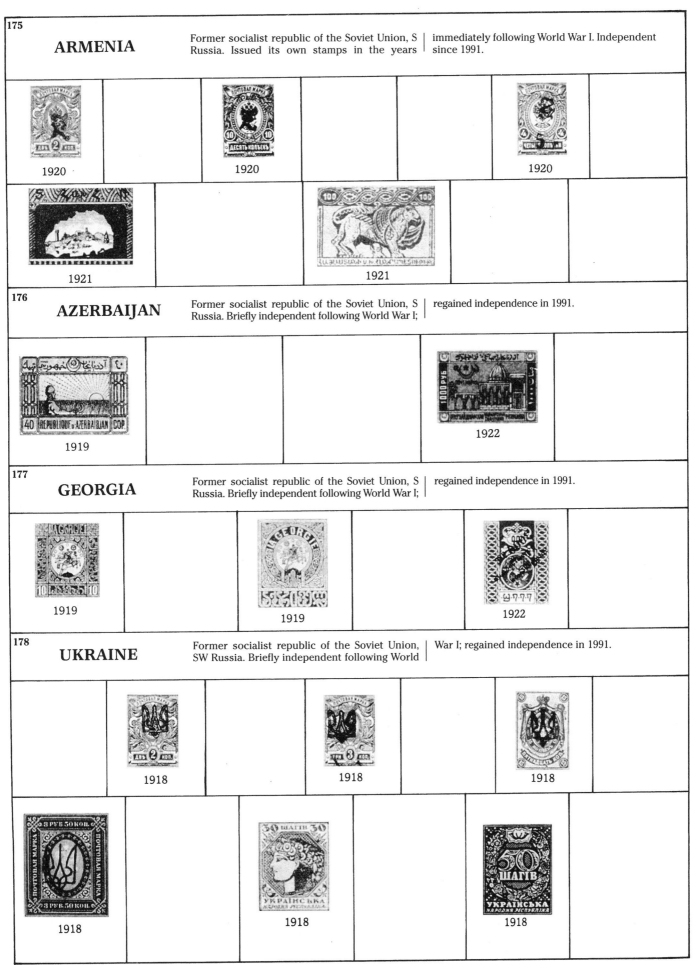

175

ARMENIA

Former socialist republic of the Soviet Union, S Russia. Issued its own stamps in the years immediately following World War I. Independent since 1991.

1920

1920

1920

1921

1921

176

AZERBAIJAN

Former socialist republic of the Soviet Union, S Russia. Briefly independent following World War I; regained independence in 1991.

1919

1922

177

GEORGIA

Former socialist republic of the Soviet Union, S Russia. Briefly independent following World War I; regained independence in 1991.

1919

1919

1922

178

UKRAINE

Former socialist republic of the Soviet Union, SW Russia. Briefly independent following World War I; regained independence in 1991.

1918

1918

1918

1918

1918

1918

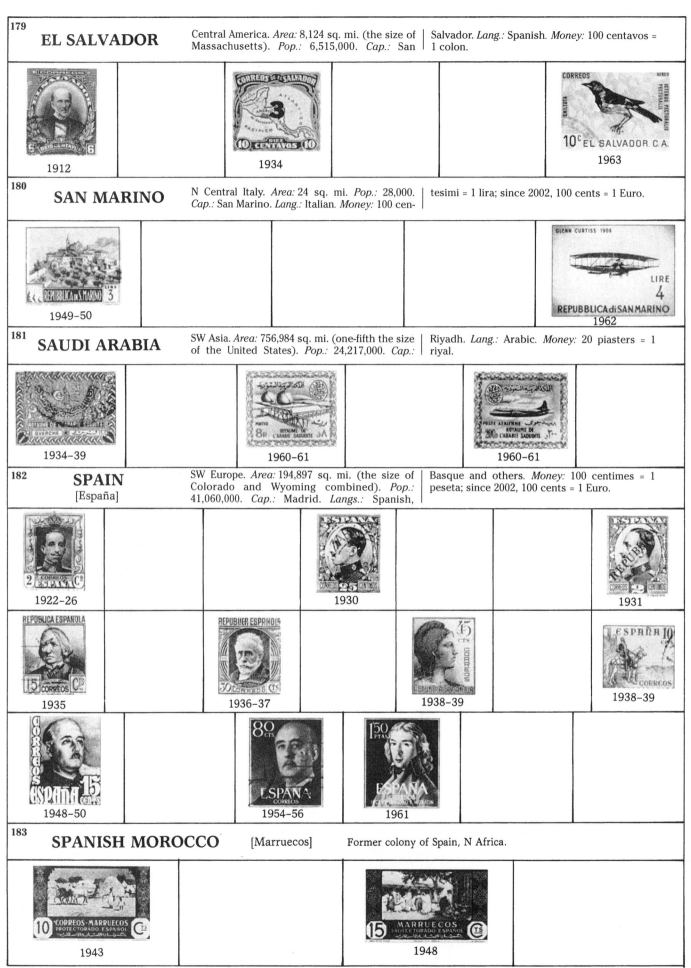

179

EL SALVADOR

Central America. *Area:* 8,124 sq. mi. (the size of Massachusetts). *Pop.:* 6,515,000. *Cap.:* San | Salvador. *Lang.:* Spanish. *Money:* 100 centavos = 1 colon.

1912   1934   1963

180

SAN MARINO

N Central Italy. *Area:* 24 sq. mi. *Pop.:* 28,000. *Cap.:* San Marino. *Lang.:* Italian. *Money:* 100 cen- | tesimi = 1 lira; since 2002, 100 cents = 1 Euro.

1949–50   1962

181

SAUDI ARABIA

SW Asia. *Area:* 756,984 sq. mi. (one-fifth the size of the United States). *Pop.:* 24,217,000. *Cap.:* | Riyadh. *Lang.:* Arabic. *Money:* 20 piasters = 1 riyal.

1934–39   1960–61   1960–61

182

SPAIN
[España]

SW Europe. *Area:* 194,897 sq. mi. (the size of Colorado and Wyoming combined). *Pop.:* 41,060,000. *Cap.:* Madrid. *Langs.:* Spanish, | Basque and others. *Money:* 100 centimes = 1 peseta; since 2002, 100 cents = 1 Euro.

1922–26   1930   1931

1935   1936–37   1938–39   1938–39

1948–50   1954–56   1961

183

SPANISH MOROCCO   [Marruecos]   Former colony of Spain, N Africa.

1943   1948

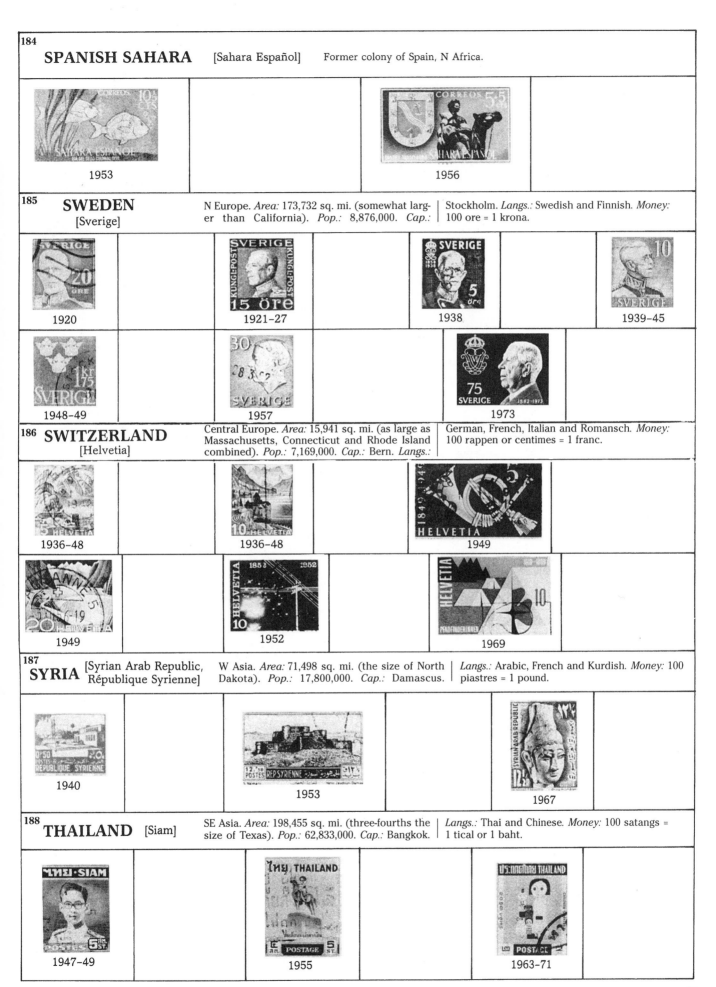

184

SPANISH SAHARA   [Sahara Español]   Former colony of Spain, N Africa.

1953		1956	

185

SWEDEN
[Sverige]

N Europe. *Area:* 173,732 sq. mi. (somewhat larger than California). *Pop.:* 8,876,000. *Cap.:* Stockholm. *Langs.:* Swedish and Finnish. *Money:* 100 ore = 1 krona.

1920	1921–27	1938	1939–45
1948–49	1957	1973	

186

SWITZERLAND
[Helvetia]

Central Europe. *Area:* 15,941 sq. mi. (as large as Massachusetts, Connecticut and Rhode Island combined). *Pop.:* 7,169,000. *Cap.:* Bern. *Langs.:* German, French, Italian and Romansch. *Money:* 100 rappen or centimes = 1 franc.

1936–48	1936–48	1949
1949	1952	1969

187

SYRIA   [Syrian Arab Republic, République Syrienne]

W Asia. *Area:* 71,498 sq. mi. (the size of North Dakota). *Pop.:* 17,800,000. *Cap.:* Damascus. *Langs.:* Arabic, French and Kurdish. *Money:* 100 piastres = 1 pound.

1940	1953	1967

188

THAILAND   [Siam]

SE Asia. *Area:* 198,455 sq. mi. (three-fourths the size of Texas). *Pop.:* 62,833,000. *Cap.:* Bangkok. *Langs.:* Thai and Chinese. *Money:* 100 satangs = 1 tical or 1 baht.

1947–49	1955	1963–71

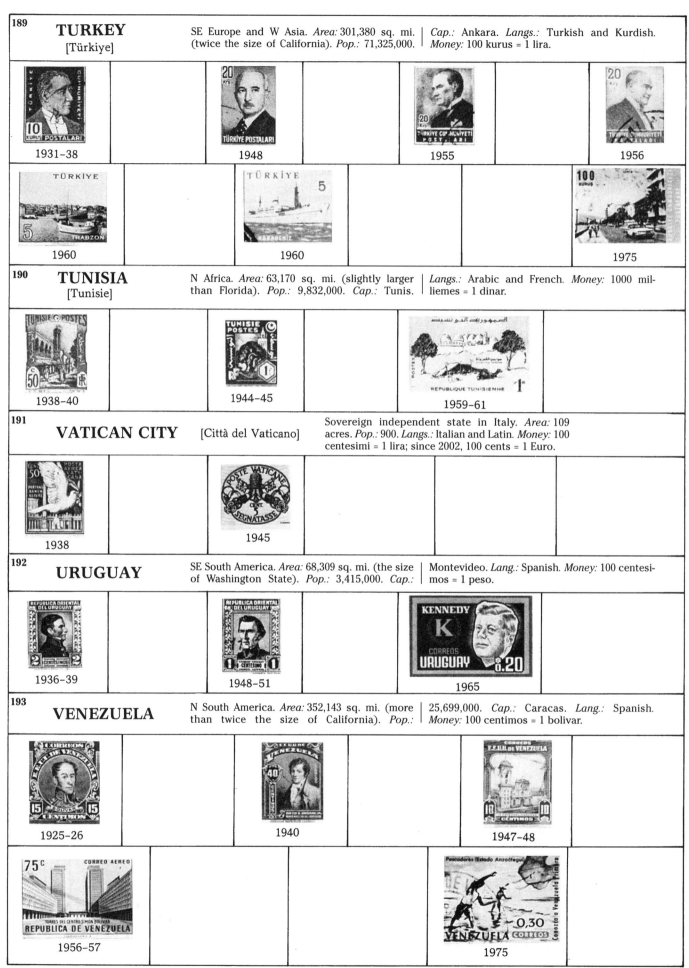

189   TURKEY

[Türkiye]

SE Europe and W Asia. *Area:* 301,380 sq. mi. (twice the size of California). *Pop.:* 71,325,000. | *Cap.:* Ankara. *Langs.:* Turkish and Kurdish. *Money:* 100 kurus = 1 lira.

1931–38	1948	1955	1956
1960	1960		1975

190   TUNISIA

[Tunisie]

N Africa. *Area:* 63,170 sq. mi. (slightly larger than Florida). *Pop.:* 9,832,000. *Cap.:* Tunis. | *Langs.:* Arabic and French. *Money:* 1000 milliemes = 1 dinar.

1938–40	1944–45	1959–61

191   VATICAN CITY   [Città del Vaticano]

Sovereign independent state in Italy. *Area:* 109 acres. *Pop.:* 900. *Langs.:* Italian and Latin. *Money:* 100 centesimi = 1 lira; since 2002, 100 cents = 1 Euro.

1938	1945	

192   URUGUAY

SE South America. *Area:* 68,309 sq. mi. (the size of Washington State). *Pop.:* 3,415,000. *Cap.:* | Montevideo. *Lang.:* Spanish. *Money:* 100 centesimos = 1 peso.

1936–39	1948–51	1965

193   VENEZUELA

N South America. *Area:* 352,143 sq. mi. (more than twice the size of California). *Pop.:* | 25,699,000. *Cap.:* Caracas. *Lang.:* Spanish. *Money:* 100 centimos = 1 bolivar.

1925–26	1940	1947–48
1956–57		1975

194 **VIETNAM**	SE Asia. *Area:* 127,244 sq. mi. (the size of New Mexico). *Pop.:* 81,377,000. *Cap.:* Hanoi. *Lang.:*	Vietnamese. *Money:* 10 francs = 1 piaster; since 1955, the dong.	

1951 | | 1951 | |

1954 | 1956 | 1957 | |

1958–59 | | 1958–59 | 1959 |

1968 | 1968 | | 1971 |

| S Arabian Peninsula. *Area:* 203,850 sq. mi. (three-fourths the size of Texas). *Pop.:* 20,010,000. *Cap.:* | Sanaa. *Lang.:* Arabic. *Money:* 40 bugshas = 1 imadi; since 1962, 40 bugshas = 1 rial. | |

1940 | | 1940 | |

Extra Pages for Special Stamps

Extra Pages for Special Stamps

Extra Pages for Special Stamps